# Gray to Gold

*For the youth of the 21st century*

**SURJIT SINGH KAVIYA**

**BLUEROSE PUBLISHERS**
India | U.K.

Copyright © Surjit Singh Kaviya 2024

All rights reserved by author. No part of this publication may be reproduced, stored in a retrieval system or transmitted in any form or by any means, electronic, mechanical, photocopying, recording or otherwise, without the prior permission of the author. Although every precaution has been taken to verify the accuracy of the information contained herein, the publisher assumes no responsibility for any errors or omissions. No liability is assumed for damages that may result from the use of information contained within.

BlueRose Publishers takes no responsibility for any damages, losses, or liabilities that may arise from the use or misuse of the information, products, or services provided in this publication.

For permissions requests or inquiries regarding this publication, please contact:

BLUEROSE PUBLISHERS
www.BlueRoseONE.com
info@bluerosepublishers.com
+91 8882 898 898
+4407342408967

ISBN: 978-93-6452-447-6

Cover design: Shivani
Typesetting: Sagar

First Edition: November 2024

*I dedicate this book to my grandfather, Mooldan Kaviya, who gifted me withsense ofhumor. To my father, Sahdev Singh Kaviya, who taught me how to thrive in hard circumstances,and to my mother, Kamala Kanwar, whose unconditional love serves as my true strength.*

# The Beginning & Acknowledgments

I had no intention of writing down my thoughts before the results of the Rajasthan Administrative Services Prelims was announced. I failed the exam despite dedicating a year and a half to its preparation. Before that result my confidence was high enough to clear all three phases of this exam. But I was eliminated in the first phase. This left me in a state of despondency. I was overwhelmed by negative thoughts and emotions.

In the coming month, I analyzed the shortcomings in my preparation which filled me with a lot of thoughts or in a state of over thinking. I found myself standing at the doorstep of anxiety and depression. I felt the emotional pressure of breaking the expectations of my family and friends. This all created a sense of guilt inside me. I was also worried about the future as it seemed ambiguous to me.

Throughout this period, I failed many times, but the journey is not asresults.The journey was awesome. At every point, I got valuable experiences and learned life hacks throughout this journey. One day, while working in my office, a thought came that I should write down my experiences so that Abhinandan, my son, could leverage them when he needs.

In the beginning, I wanted to summarize my experiences and learned insights only in ten pages. But as I crossed that limit, I realized there was much more to share. So I continued writing. After completing around forty pages, I firstacknowledged the possibility of writing a book. Although I had no ambition to become a writer. During this time, my best friends Samarth and Rajsa encouraged me to proceed further. This is how I decided and wrote down my experiences, and this book, Gray to Gold came into existence.

In this journey of writing my book, many of my well-wishers have played a vital role. Some provided me with emotional support, while others served as the backbone of intellectual guidance. My family, whose contribution to both my life and this book is immeasurable. My Wife Dipti is a constant source of positivity for me. My elder brother Gajendra singh is always backbone for me. Kuldeep Bangara, a colleague, is part of the small circle I formed for important discussions regarding writing this book. Bhavesh also supported this project in every way possible. He was available for any conversation, anytime and anywhere. I wish to express my heartfelt gratitude to my teachers, whose efforts and support have enabled me to write this book.

I am deeply grateful to all my brothers and friends, They have contributed to this journey of writing this book. I feel immense gratitude to Narpat charan, Mount Abu and Vinay Gupta, Sumerpur for opening doors to the future possibilities. I am deeply grateful to Hinglaj dan and Siddharth Charan for their invaluable contribution and steadfast support throughout this journey. All my colleagues were always ready to assist me in any way, especially Hemlata choudhary, Principal and Dharmendra Gehlot sir. The discussions I had with the students of the school, i am currently working at, significantly shaped the outline of this book. I am sincerely thankful to Shradha Arha for guiding me onto the path of writing and publishing. Everyone of them has provided unwavering support throughout this process. I feel immensely humbled and fortunate to have all of them as a part of a huge support system.

I would like to express my sincere thanks to the entire team at Blue Rose Publication for their support and cooperation. Special thanks to Consultant Sara, Publishing manager Deepika, Editor Shreya jain, Sunidhi and Ritesh for the illustrations, Sagar for formatting and to Shivani for designing a stunning book cover. Your efforts have truly brought this project to life.

Thank you Everyone, Thank you Universe

# Introduction

Welcome You to: Gray to Gold, a transformative way designed to empower the new generation. The 21st century is an era of uncertainties, unprecedented changes, rapid technological advancements, and complex global challenges. In this time, the younger generation is facing challenges that demand a new set of skills. This book is a bundle of these essential skills. It will provide the crucial knowledge and insights necessary to navigate the coming time. Believe in yourself and get ready to become the updated version of yourself, which is the must fulfilling requirement of this time.

The 21st century is an era of unique opportunities and challenges. On one hand, developments in technology have opened doors to possibilities that were unimaginable just a few decades ago. On the other hand, these same technological advancements have brought about new challenges. The pressure to succeed in such an environment can lead youth to stress and exploitation.

There are many ways to live life. Some are worthy; some are futile, some are effortless; some are arduous, some are purposeful; some are meaningless, some are useful; some are fatal, some are magical; some are real, some are right; some are wrong, some are lawful; some are lawless, some are for life; some are against it. The way consists of our actions and reactions, our attitude and aptitude, our habits and patterns, our behaviour and character, our decisions and choices, our yeses and no's. The Way is how we play and perform, sense and express, use and utilize, connect and communicate, care and control, move and flow, recharge and regain, think and feel, prefer and prioritize, accept and resist. The way is the thing which shapes our life. The way we choose defines our lives. For an easy, effortless, meaningful, useful and magical life, the only compulsory thing is to use the right way.

History is full of examples highlighting the consequences of choosing the wrong path or making wrong decisions. This book suggests fruitful "Gray to Gold" ways for a better life.

This book is structured into 39 chapters. Each of these chapters is addressing a distinct but crucial concept. Every chapter discusses a specific issue and offers practical solutions and actionable advice to turn obstacles into opportunities. This comprehensive approach ensures that readers can find the best possible solutions to the diverse problems of their lives.

The core techniques of this book are enough to turn your gray personality into a golden one. The book illustrates the best tricks and techniques to overcome various adversities. By learning these time tested methods, you can develop a set of skills that can transform your gray areas into golden virtues.

Another significant focus of this book is the battle against distractions. The digital era comes with the distractions that can derail focus and productivity. This book provides strategies for managing distractions and creating a balanced life. By mastering the skills mentioned in the book, you can reclaim your time and energy.

The pressures of modern life often lead to the negligence of physical and mental health. Health is the foundation of survivability and success. This book emphasizes the importance of holistic well-being. It offers many tips on maintaining a healthy lifestyle. You can prioritize self-love and self-care by following the tips in the book. You can build a strong foundation of sound health that will support your ambitions and aspirations.

Each chapter is going to level you up on the journey of your personal and professional growth. This book equips the youth with the tools they need to navigate the complexities of the modern world. It is a call-to-action for you to take charge of your life. You must recognize your potential and transform the adversities of today into the achievements of tomorrow.

The book also provides basic survival knowledge in the complex and uncertain nature of human's social and individual life. Social structures are developed with passing time and play a crucial role in our lives. Understanding and using these structures make life smoother. But if you dare to go against them, it may result in undesired consequences.

Always remember that every challenge you face is a hidden opportunity. This book is your true companion in this journey. It offers you true wisdom, time-tested techniques, and practical pieces of advice to help you turn the gray areas of your life into golden capabilities. I acknowledge that my words may not fully capture these broad concepts. I encourage you to apply your logic and intelligence to enhance the potential of this book. I express my gratitude to you for holding these pages. You bring to life my vision Gray to Gold.

# How to Read the Book

This book, Gray to Gold, is designed for the overall well-being of the reader. As the name suggests, the purpose of this book is to transform the reader's gray personality into a golden one. After completing the journey through this book, the rust from your personality will disappear, and you will rise to a golden personality. For maximum results, I would like to offer you some suggestions for reading this book.

This book comprises of 39 chapters, and each of them is intended to guide you on the right path of living. Every line of every paragraph is filled with useful information. I request you to maintain a slow reading pace so that you can observe the hidden treasure within the words. I also advise you to dedicate two to three days, reading 15–20 minutes per day, to complete every chapter. While reading this book, remember that your goal is not only to finish it but to extract the maximum insights and incorporate them into your life. As soon as apply these tricks and techniques you learn from the chapters, so these can be a part of your behaviour.

I have structured this book in a way to effortlessly create a strong personality. This book will help you to become the best and updated version of yourself. At the end of each chapter, you will get self-affirmations related to the chapter. These are designed to instil real values in your personality through training your subconscious part of brain. Along with this, each chapter has its image or sketch to create a stable mental image related to the topic or concept.

In the future, if you sense that you have lost insights which you learned from this book, I advise you to revisit it to refresh your understanding and memory. Feel free to discuss this book with your friends and family to get deeper into its teachings and insights.

# Contents

Awareness of Affirmations ............................................................. 1

Art of Repairing ............................................................................ 6

Miracles of Acceptance ................................................................ 10

Springboard of Good Habits Grid ................................................ 16

Slow and steady .......................................................................... 23

Embrace Self-care ....................................................................... 28

Flow in Flow State ...................................................................... 32

Break Rigidity ............................................................................. 36

Reaction Rules ............................................................................ 42

Right Here and Right Now .......................................................... 46

Living with Less .......................................................................... 50

Happy Parents Are the Best Parents ............................................ 54

Break Free from Addiction .......................................................... 60

Worship your Work ..................................................................... 66

Say No to Vultures ...................................................................... 70

Grow in Nature ........................................................................... 76

You with Resources ..................................................................... 81

Power of Ignorance ..................................................................... 87

Foundation of Friendship ............................................................ 92

High Five Way ............................................................................ 98

Shadow of sexual behviour ........................................................ 102

Accept, Stop and Create Change ............................................... 109

Life is Colourful ........................................................................ 114

| | |
|---|---|
| You, Your Choices and Your Destiny | 119 |
| Relax to Regain | 122 |
| You with Others | 125 |
| Overview of Social Media | 130 |
| Find out Patterns | 134 |
| You are Unique | 137 |
| Hunting Pleasure or Self | 141 |
| What feels Negative is not necessarily negative | 144 |
| Smart Speaking | 147 |
| Impress Yourself | 151 |
| Safeguard secrets | 154 |
| Money Matters | 157 |
| Path of Gratitude | 163 |
| Inhale and Exhale | 167 |
| Books Worth Reading | 170 |
| Movies Worth Watching | 176 |

# Awareness of Affirmations

*"Your beliefs become your thoughts, your thoughts become your words, your words become your actions, your actions become your habits, your habits become your values, and your values become your destiny." - Mahatma Gandhi*

We give significant importance to our conversation with others. We often overlook the significance of our internal dialogue, the conversation with self. The majority of people underestimate its importance and its potential side effects. Let me first clarify the concept of the mind. The mind is different from the brain. The mind is not a part of you. You are not your mind. The mind is a collection or cloud of negative thoughts, feelings and emotions. The mind is not stable because these mental aspects are not permanent. This is your biggest confusion: that you wrongly identify yourself with your mind.

You make the mistakes when you consider what your mind suggests.

Thinking that your mind defines you is a real big problem. The mind use thoughts, feelings and emotions to confuse your brain and body. It acts like an unwanted companion. The mind is like a parasite. When you get lost in thoughts and emotions for too long, the mind gains more control over your brain and body. You can become addicted to this mental state and after doing what the mind dictates.

Here, I would also like to introduce the concept of consciousness. Consciousness represents your true nature. It is the best coordination state between your brain and body. In this state, your senses and your actions synchronize. Consciousness and the mind are opposites. Consciousness brings positive elements like safety, security, success, genuine joy, happiness, and connection with the present. In contrast, the mind tends to do the opposite. Consciousness is a state of alertness, awareness, and activeness. The mind is a state of insensibility, over thinking and inactiveness. Consciousness is genuine and good. The mind is deceptive and dangerous. Consciousness works for you. The mind works against you.

Here, my intention is to clarify the concepts of the mind and consciousness so that it will be easier for you to understand your internal dialogue with consciousness and the mind. Both communicates with you. It is your choice whose voice you choose to listen to. A smart and intelligent person tends to lean toward the side of consciousness. A fool and emotional creature may choose the path that is led by the mind. From now on, I will use "conversation with self" for both the conversation with consciousness and the mind to avoid confusion.

In our conversations with self or others, we tend to accept some things as true and reject others. When you accept or believe something to be true, it becomes an affirmation. Affirmations play a crucial role in shaping your personality, behaviour and life to a large extent. There are two types of affirmations, positive and negative. Positive affirmations are statements that benefit you. They make you feel strong and attract positive outcomes. On the other hand, negative affirmations are harmful. They create obstacles in your holistic development and hinder your progress. Therefore, it's crucial to understand that your affirmations shape your beliefs. Ultimately, you become what you believe. You must choose positive affirmations to contribute to your well-being and success. You must keep yourself away from negative affirmations because it can have detrimental effects on your personal and professional life. Now I am going to suggest you some "Gray to Gold" ways to use affirmations as a helpful tool and avoid them as a self-harming weapon.

The most important thing to always listen to your consciousness. Don't allow your mind to suggest anything. Stay in present and prevent the mind from growing.

Never affirm anything negative. Always affirm positive things.

Avoid affirming anything negative about your capabilities, strengths, and skills. Always say yes to positive affirmations regarding the mentioned aspects.

Don't judge others or affirm anything wrong about anybody. Be clear and thoughtful when you are making or expressing judgments.

Observe wrong things from a safe distance. You should only engage and experience the positive things.

Don't let others set your beliefs. Your beliefs should originate directly from your consciousness.

Question the beliefs that prevails in society. You must pass them through your consciousness. You should believe what your consciousness suggests.

Acknowledge that everyone has unique beliefs. There is no universal belief. It's okay if someone has different beliefs from yours.

Don't let the advertising industry, social media, and the virtual world manipulate your beliefs.

Only affirm what's positive, truthful, and beneficial for you.

## Self-Affirmations

I am............................................. and I affirm positivity in every aspect of my life. My consciousness guides me to affirm only positive things. I consciously reject any negative thoughts and beliefs. I don't let my mind create chaos by affirming negativity in my life. I am in control of my thoughts. I affirm only what uplifts and empowers me. Every affirmation I make adds value to my well-being and success. I attract positivity by affirming the good in myself and others. I consciously shape a positive life.

*"Affirmations are a powerful tool to deliberately install desired beliefs about yourself." - Nikki Carnevale*

# Art of Repairing

*"The only way to fix a broken heart is time, patience, and unconditional love." - Unknown*

There is a difference between fixable and non-fixable things. Fixable things can be repaired if broken, while non-fixable things cannot. The skill of repairing is one of the best skills you can have. It provides stability and strength throughout life. Life is fragile, but having the skill of repairing it, everything becomes easy.

So many challenges come in life, some of them are easy to handle, but some of them are very painful. It requires an understanding of the unique ways to fix various aspects of life. Thus, repairing becomes a crucial skill in dealing with hard times.

We start by exploring the ways of repairing visible things. Instruments we use at home or school may break and need to be repaired. Most effective repair demands practice, the right tools, focused attention, patience, and full devotion to restoring items to their best condition. A good working environment and sometimes human resources may also be required. I also emphasize the importance of planning and organizing abilities.

Now is the time to consider the repairing of invisible things. For example, a misunderstanding with your best friend can ruin your friendship. Repairing invisible aspects of our lives require a different approach. The main tool here you must use is communication. Communication is a vital component in restoring relationships. Healthy communication is very important for nurturing and maintaining social life. In the chapters related to human behaviour and art of speaking, I had discussed enough about the fundamental principles of communication.

Now we are going to repair an important part of life, that is health. Suppose your health deteriorates due to weight gain. Repairing your health involves some basic factors like analyzing the situation and creating a proper plan. This plan could include physical activities like running, jogging, playing, and dietary considerations. Discipline, willpower, interest, and patience are also crucial for executing the plan to restore your health.

Now is the time for your studies. Suppose your academic performance suffers due to some circumstances. There is no need to be sad about past results. Now you must repair your presenting order to create a good future. Here you have to repair the pattern you follow for studying. Repairing your study pattern may involve analyzing past shortcomings, creating a new plan, developing good habits, and managing time effectively. If you follow the appropriate way to repair your academic performance, you will get amazing results.

Most important is how you deal with hard times. Repairing these hard times through various skills becomes inevitable because if you do not do so, it has enough potential for creating a mess in your life. Building good relations, maintaining a positive attitude, accepting what cannot be changed, focusing on creativity, staying optimistic, and practicing self-care without guilt are crucial for safely going through hard times. You cannot ignore the severity of hard times, because it can have long-lasting negative effects on your life. Every challenge should be addressed at the right time in the right way.

Learning to repair is not only a practical skill, but also it's a philosophy that makes our life easy. It removes life's unwanted burdens and increases happiness. It also maintains order in our lives. So, embrace the art of repair— it's the way to make life easier, creative, and more meaningful.

## Self-Affirmations

I am………………………………………….. and I possess the skills to repair visible or invisible things. Every broken thing is an opportunity for me to empower my repairing abilities. My dedication to learning and practicing repair techniques is awesome. Misunderstandings are opportunities for me to strengthen relationships through repair. I approach repairing relations with empathy and understanding. I feel positive when I repair the intangible aspects of my life. I always keep monitoring my health and repair if it needed. I always monitor my studies and repair and fix any broken schedule. I am a master of the art of repairing.

> *"Sometimes the best way to fix a broken relationship is to remember why it started in the first place." - Unknown*

# Miracles of Acceptance

*"Acceptance looks like a passive state, but in reality, it brings something entirely new into this world. That peace, a subtle energy vibration, is consciousness." - Eckhart Tolle*

People often talk about how life is tough. To prove that, they share examples of difficulties and struggles. Sometimes, we get stuck in negative thoughts and emotions, and we start thinking that life is hard. When we try to overcome tough situations, we may feel some bad feelings like pain, anxiety, and sadness. I want to make it clear that it's not the difficult times but the resentment we develop for the hard times that cause all this negativity. The main reason for any sorrow is the resentment or bitterness toward certain situations or people. It's important to understand about resentment and acceptance. Then only you can understand how you handle challenges or people in your life. Only then you will understand how you are shaping your life.

Resentment is a feeling of strong dislike. It comes when you believe that you have been treated unfairly. It doesn't have just one cause. Resentment happens when you think someone or something has treated you badly or unfairly. Mostly, it is because of misunderstandings or not seeing the full picture. In simple words, resentment means not accepting things as they are. Your mind plays a tricky role in this. It uses fake examples and wrong facts to make you feel negative about someone or something. The mind creates all the negativity by introducing resentment in your life. Resentment has enough potential to cause you severe losses. That is why it becomes very important to understand how it affects you and your life.

Resentment drains positive energy from you and fills your brain and body with negativity. This negativity hinders you from doing anything productive. When your reservoir of positive energy is depleted, it becomes challenging for positive things to happen in your life. The vacancy of positive things invites negative things into your life.

If you have too much resentment, it is detrimental to your health. It can cause physical problems like illness. It can make you vulnerable to any disease and can disrupt your body's normal functions. If we talk about mental health, it can leads to stress, anxiety, and depression. Resentment can also harm your relationships by lowering your social status. It can weaken your support system from friends and family. That is why resentment is like carrying around a heavy burden. Not only it affects how you feel inside, but it also influences your overall well-being including your relationships with others. Here I want to mention some of the detrimental impacts of resentment on your life.

The path of resentment is self-destructive. It only harms you and your overall well-being.

Resentment can destabilize your life. It can lead you to significant financial losses. It negatively impacts your earning capacity and that results in your poor financial choices.

This negative emotion keeps you away from joy and happiness. It makes you feel constantly sad.

If you are consumed by resentment, you will miss the opportunities. It negatively impacts various aspects of your life.

Your learning capabilities will decline as your senses weaken under the weight of resentment. Resentment makes it challenging to acquire new skills or knowledge.

I believe we've discussed resentment sufficiently. Now, it's time to explore the way out of resentment. On the flip side of resentment, there is always acceptance to lend you a helping hand. Acceptance acts as a remedy for the ailments caused by resentment. Acceptance works like magic. It's potential to transform anything negative into positive is magical and unbelievable. Experiencing the power of acceptance is truly awesome. The feeling of acceptance is one of the best experiences you can have in your life.

Acceptance is quite simple, it is not as complex as resentment. It is within everyone's reach. We all must be thankful for its straightforward nature. Regarding this chapter, acceptance has two meanings, and they are…

The first meaning is clear: " Accept anything as it is". It's about acknowledging that whatever comes to us, we should accept them without any feeling of change. Life itself is full of changes. We all must accept the truth that nothing is permanent. Everything will change when the right time comes. This belief will add beauty to your journey. If you succeed in developing a habit of seeing the positive side of things, it will help you face challenges and hard times without any struggle.

The second meaning is simple: "Without resentment". If something needs to be changed, go ahead and make the changes. But remember, do it without having any hard feelings or strong dislike. You need to work for both creating and stopping changes. In situations where a reaction is needed, you must respond without carrying any resentment. For example, If you have to fight, do it, but don't have negative feelings or resentment for your opponent. It's all about learning to act without resentment to work against you.

Earlier, we discussed the harms of resentment. Now we will explore the benefits of acceptance. I will share just a few of the immense advantages of acceptance.

Acceptance simplifies your journey through hard times. It makes hard times less arduous.

It purifies your thoughts, feelings, and emotions. It cleanses our brain and body. Unfinished matters live as residue in our minds, which can cause a lack of concentration and other serious issues. Acceptance allows us to release this residue.

Acceptance keeps you in the present moment. Acceptance strengthens your senses.

It diminishes negativity, sadness, and pain by its magical power. You can experience yourself. Acceptance is amazing at doing this.

Acceptance is an energy-saving mode for your brain and body. It directs your energy toward positive things in your life.

It connects you to the great energy source, that is Universe. When you embrace acceptance, the whole universe starts supporting you.

Acceptance cures your physical and psychological illness caused by resentment. Acceptance provides you with healing without medication.

Adopting an accepting behaviour attracts others. It creates a likeable personality. You can attract people by being a strong magnet of acceptance.

Acceptance is your true nature. It provides you with long-lasting inner peace and happiness.

By embracing acceptance, you can unlock doors to new opportunities.

## Self-Affirmations

I am................ and I embrace the power of acceptance in my life. I let go of any type of resentment. Negativity has no place in my thoughts, feelings, and emotions. I choose to focus on the positive aspects of everything. I release all resentment and allow acceptance to guide my journey. I am grateful for all the benefits acceptance brings to me. Each day I choose acceptance over resentment. I feel inner peace and joy by walking on the path of acceptance.

*"Happiness can exist only in acceptance."* - George Orwell

# Springboard of Good Habits Grid

*"Motivation is what gets you started. Habit is what keeps you going." - Jim Ryun*

We have a lot of work to do each day and find it hard to concentrate much on a specific task because we also need to stay aware of other activities around us. There is no need to worry, Mother Nature has blessed us with the ability to multitask and play different roles simultaneously. We perform tasks perfectly even when not fully focused, for example, driving. It seems our brain and body have special functions to take control effortlessly in certain situations when we need our focus or concentration on something else.

Sometimes, it also feels like our body has its own memory. It doesn't require any active support from the conscious thinking while performing a specific task. Have you observed an expert performing a task in a particular field? If you did so, you would have noticed their skills, speed, and mind-blowing body movements. Every day, we perform so many automatic tasks, such as brushing our teeth or cycling a familiar route. This ability allows our brains to avoid being overwhelmed by concentrating on each detail.

After knowing all this, a simple question will arise in your mind. What makes all that possible? The answer is "The basal ganglia. It is the part of our brain and is situated deep in the forebrain. It controls voluntary movements of our body. It plays a critical role in how people form habits, both bad and good. Here, our task is to learn about habits. Let's learn.

Habits are the automatic actions we perform every day. On average, 40 percent of our behaviour per day consists of habits. It makes habit a crucial part of our lives. Your current life is the sum of your habits. Whether you are happy or unhappy, successful or unsuccessful, I can say it is the result of your habits. Whatever actions you repeatedly do each day, shapes your beliefs, and your personality. Therefore, habits constitute 40 percent of your life. By developing good habits and eliminating bad ones, you can effectively manage 40 percent portion of your life. That is why you should take habits seriously and start working on them.

Habits are all about repetition. Whatever we repeat again and again forms a habit. Each repetition strengthens a habit. Developing good habits requires intentional repetition. For doing so, it needs willpower, strict discipline, and a reward and punishment or carrot-and-stick policy. It is also important to note the distinction between good and bad habits. Good habits bring positive physical, emotional, or psychological benefits and make our lives easier. On the other hand, bad habits result in negative consequences. Bad habits only create problems in our lives. Positive habits contribute to success, while bad habits are responsible for hard times.

Our habits are the reflection of our choices. Habits and choices are interconnected with each other. One good habit supports other good habits and weakens bad habits. One bad habit strengthens other bad habits and weakens good habits. Habits create an intertwined grid of good or bad. Good habits form a supportive grid, while bad habits create a grid that is harmful to us. It is up to us which grid we nurture the most. Through positive affirmations and conscious repetition, you can to instil good habits. Here, I suggest 21" Gray to Gold" habits to create a favourable grid in the 21st century.

Make it a habit to get up early in the morning. You must be a member of the early riser club. This good habit is the foundation of all positive habits. This habit offers the best start to your day. When you are prepared for the day before the sun rises, it will make you feel that you respect the importance of the day. This habit may take 2-3 months to become ingrained in your mind. But the benefits of this wonderful habit you will get throughout life are immense. It provides you with extra hours and an advantage over others.

When you get up in the morning, develop the habit of making your bed. It becomes the first accomplishment of the day and motivates you to do more tasks. This simple act boosts your energy and interest and keeps you active throughout the day. This increased interest in your work leads to positive outcomes. The habit of making your bed daily is a wonderful example of how small actions can change your life.

Be grateful for what you have and what you receive. Show gratitude for life, health, opportunities, happy moments, parents, good friends, and the success you have achieved. The list is endless. Express gratitude for even the smallest positive things that happen to you. Being grateful is your responsibility, so make it a habit to show your gratitude.

Be conscious and aware at all times. Avoid over thinking and don't allow your mind to wander. Open up all your senses and gradually strengthen them through constant use.

Practice being in the present moment. Stay connected to your surroundings by being here and now. Your world is what you can sense. Don't create an imaginary world. Don't wander in the past or future. Make it a habit to be here and now.

Form the habit of affirming positive things. Affirmations play a vital role in shaping your life. Always be conscious and aware of what you affirm to yourself and make it a habit.

Create the habit of confidently saying 'Yes or No'. Use 'Yes or No' as your directive tool. It will provide a suitable direction to your life based on circumstances. Through this habit you will have full control of your life.

Be a humble person. With this habit, you become less selfish and more inclined toward the feelings and emotions of others. You should find joy in others' success. Don't feel jealous or be arrogant. This is how you will be able to build stronger relationships.

Develop the habit of working with interest. Your work is crucial for your survival. There should be no resentment in doing any work. When an uncertain task comes your way, don't see it as a burden, but as an opportunity.

Prepare a specific pattern for each task, then repeat it to create a habit. By doing daily tasks with habitual patterns, you can decrease mental burden and save both energy and time.

Start journaling daily and make it a habit. Journaling is a gateway to self-exploration. It allows you to track your personal growth, understand emotions, and boost memory. It also enhances self-discipline and communication skills. Dedicate a few minutes each day to write down thoughts, ideas, and emotions. Very soon you will notice the immense benefits.

Physical activity is essential for your health and overall well-being. You can start with 15 minutes of easy exercises like walking, jogging, and yoga. You can gradually increase time and intensity of your exercises. Be kind to your body when you are going to start building this habit.

The old saying "you are what you eat" is very important in shaping your eating habits. Your diet impacts your physical and mental health. Avoid fast food and unhealthy options. Instead, you can include more organic food, vegetables, and fruits. Experiment with preparing healthy and delicious meals and increase your knowledge about the nutritional value of various foods.

Reading is a valuable habit. Be a regular reader. Reading newspapers is essential for staying updated on geopolitics, technology, and other global events. Books also upgrade your knowledge. Be a voracious reader and develop the habit of reading. This is how you gain the knowledge required in this era.

Always listen to both sides before you are going to judge anything. One-sided perspective is dangerous because it's a half and incomplete view of something. Like every coin has two sides, everything has its pros and cons. Before reaching any conclusions you must be aware of everything related to the particular matter.

Your company plays an important role in shaping your personality. Learn from your friends. You must have good companions to elevate your status. Choose friends who prioritize their work and understand the value of time.

Maintain order in your surroundings. You can start by putting your shoes in order. External order brings internal order, and internal order brings external order. Order brings you both satisfaction and peace.

Intake slowly, whether it is breathing, drinking, eating, and learning. The best and most effective way to intake anything is to be slow. Develop the habit of doing these activities slowly.

Stay cool and calm in any situation. Avoid overexcitement when you are happy, sad, and angry. If you practice being cool and calm you can turn circumstances into opportunities.

Love yourself. To achieve success, self-love is necessary. There is a difference between self-care and selfishness. It is your responsibility to take care of yourself, your body and your life. Love yourself to enhance your capabilities and confidence. Make self-love a habit and stop blaming yourself for anything that is not in your control.

Don't take life seriously. Life is uncertain. It is like a water bubble. Accept whatever comes your way. There is no absolute right or wrong. Life is paradoxical so don't waste time trying to solve it. Instead, you should live, enjoy, and experience new tastes of life. Play your role in this drama without taking life too seriously.

## Self-Affirmations

I am................................. and I welcome good habits into my life with open arms. I never break good habits. I strengthen and reinforce good habits consistently. My daily choices align with supportive and healthy habits. I embrace a lifestyle that encourages and sustains healthy habits. I am aware of the opportunities to incorporate good habits into my daily routine. I am mindful of the constructive or destructive power of habits. I am the master of my habits.

*"We first make our habits, and then our habits make us."*
*- John Dryden*

# Slow and steady

*"Slow down and everything you are chasing will come around and catch you." - John De Paola*

This is the first time in history that humans have an abundance of things. It all happened because of evolution. Everyone is obsessed with the idea of getting more. This has become part of how humans think. The world of today is shaped by this force – the desire of humans to get more. This desire can create, destroy, manipulate, and exploit anything. And the sad part is that it seems like the desire for more has stolen people's joy and happiness. People are so focused on getting more that they forget to stop and relax. They keep running in the same routine every day. After working hard all day, they feel exhausted and sad.

This is also the first time in human history that people have so many desires, wishes, and a lot of things to possess. The excess of everything has created a complex and never-ending rat race for all human beings. People do not think about what they are doing and where they are going. Unfortunately, this is the new normal of our society. No one is thinking wrong about this rat race, but everyone who is running knows he is suffering.

A person has to compromise so many things while running after materialistic possessions. The most valuable thing compromised is time. We have a limited amount of time because we cannot produce more time. We do not have any control over passing time. We spend our most valuable resource, which is time, on less valuable things. We realize its importance when our limit is almost finished. Wasting time is the biggest self-created loss. Along with time, our busyness damages our health, relationships, inner peace, dreams, and desires.

Now is the time to discuss the magical way to deal with the problems created by our busyness. You are going to learn about the importance of "learning to be slow". Our society suggests being fast to compete with others for status and security. This is a very narrow perspective. It leaves many dimensions of our lives untouched. For a healthy, wealthy, and happy life, all aspects need proper attention, time, energy, and efforts. You cannot manage all the fundamental aspects of life altogether by being fast. But this magical tool will make you capable of dealing with all aspects of life altogether in the best way. Whatever we do requires focus, energy, and time. It can only be achieved by slowing down to cover all aspects. Being slow allows you to use all your senses together by staying in the present. Any work done perfectly gives a sense of satisfaction. Enjoyment and fun come when one does work with full engagement. Here are a few ways to apply this tool....

- ➢ Getting excited is good for work. But if you are too excited, it can create a mess. So, it is better not to get overly excited. Just stay slow and aware for better results in whatever you are doing.

- ➢ When you start, first go slow to make sure you don't miss anything of less or more importance. Then you can speed up gradually. This is how you should pay attention to details and smoothly increase your pace when you work.

- ➢ When you are doing any tasks try to identify moments when you need to be slow and fast. It will ensure you can complete your work effectively.

- ➢ When you eat, don't rush. Chew your food slowly and make sure to swallow it only after chewing it well. This helps your body digest the food properly. You will get more energy. Eating slowly with awareness makes the whole experience better for your health.

- ➢ When you breathe, go slow. Inhale and exhale deeply and slowly start it from your stomach. This mindful breathing promotes relaxation and calms your brain and body. Slow and deep breaths contribute to overall well-being. It reduces stress and enhances a sense of calmness in your life.

- ➢ When you study, don't hurry. Take your time to understand and learn. This is how you can get the most out of your studies by being mindful and slow. You can learn and remember things better.

➢ When you are riding a bike or driving a car, go slow to keep full control and prevent accidents. Being slow and cautious ensures a safe journey. Take your time and enjoy the trip. You can only appreciate the surroundings by keeping your speed moderate. Going at a slow pace not only enhances your safety but also adds to the pleasure of your travel experience.

➢ Don't overreact. The way you respond is crucial. Be precise and take your time to react thoughtfully. Your responses are more important than the initial action. Taking enough time to respond can lead to more effective reactions.

➢ When you speak, be to the point and slow, and people will pay attention and give importance to your words. You should take care to be slow and precise in your communication. This is the best way you can express yourself. It can have a significant impact on others. You must always speak with clarity. This will ensure better understanding and enhances the value of your message.

Being slow is like having a relaxed moment. It is like meditation. It brings genuine joy and meaning to life. Your work gets better, and you feel more productive. You have a limited time, so find happiness going along with the pace of time. Being slow is not about stopping and doing nothing, instead, it is about being mindful in every moment. When you sync up with time, a deep sense of fulfilment comes to you. You can turn the limited time into a colourful and purposeful experience of living. So, enjoy the journey by being slow and aware.

## Self-Affirmations

I am ………………………….. and I eat each bite slowly and mindfully. I give my body the time it needs for completing any task. I take slow and deep breaths. I find calmness and presence with every inhale and exhale. I do my studies with patience. I take full time to understand and learn what I am studying. I respond and react thoughtfully. I always consider controlled actions and reactions. I drive and ride at a slow and steady pace. I ensure a safe and relaxed journey. I begin tasks slowly for its accurate execution. I live my life with Joy and happiness by being slow and aware.

*"Slow down and enjoy life. It's not only the scenery you miss by going too fast – you also miss the sense of where you are going and why." - Eddie Cantor*

# Embrace Self-care

*"Don't sacrifice yourself too much, because if you sacrifice too much, there's nothing else you can give, and nobody will care for you." - Karl Lagerfeld*

Our personality development determines how successful a life we will have. Personality development has many key factors that play an important role in shaping it. The main key factors are genetics, family atmosphere, social atmosphere, and self-care. Many of them you cannot control, but what you can do is practice self-care. As other factors hold control over your life, it is through self-care that you can try to regain it. Self-care is your tool through which you can shape your personality to achieve the desired future. It is through self-love and self-care that you can express your gratitude to God for the life He has given you.

You will encounter many people in your life. Some will accept you as you are. Many people will try to change you to fit in their lives. They aim to shape you for their benefit. They will make decisions on your behalf, and they will manipulate you with their cleverness and wisdom. In doing so, they seek to establish control over you.

Fear plays a significant role in holding us back. It causes our dreams and desires to be unfulfilled. The joy and happiness we seek appear distant. In that condition, self-love is replaced by self-hatred and self-care is substituted with self-demolition. This is how a beautiful life without self-love and self-care becomes like a plant without water.

The people will keep trying to mould you into something you don't fit. The impact of others decisions can be detrimental for you. It can lead to a sense of loss and self-sabotage. It is essential to recognize the importance of self-care in nurturing your overall well-being. It will also help in maintaining a sense of uniqueness in the face of external pressures. Only through self-love and genuine self-care, you can truly flourish and lead a happy and fulfilling life.

There is a significant difference between selfishness and self-care. Since life is given to us with the responsibility to take care of it, it requires keeping control of your life in your hands. Do not allow anyone to dictate your life or shape you according to their wishes. If anyone with bad intentions tries to manipulate you, then clearly and firmly say to him, "I am who I am, accept me or leave me". This declaration will create a protective layer around you. It will communicate to manipulators that you cannot be moulded according to their desires. It will set boundaries to safeguard your individuality and autonomy. That is how you must acknowledge your right to self-care. That is how you can be free from external pressures. You should always remember that your well-being and self-worth are only your priorities. The self-care is the tool that will empower you to honour your priorities.

Here I am not suggesting that you should not change. Change is an important part of our lives. It is okay to change with time and circumstances, but it's not okay to change what suits others. I would like to mention that it's a broad concept; don't use it in a narrow perspective. Flexibility is also crucial. For smaller issues, it's okay to be flexible. Smaller issues are those that don't have much effect on your holistic well-being. They do not impact your self-care. With family, friends, and sometimes even strangers, it is okay to compromise on smaller things.

But when it comes to broader issues, you must show rigidity. Broader issues are those that can severely affect your overall well-being. They can lead you to significant losses. Broader issues can compromise your self-respect. It can negatively impacts your psychological, emotional, and physical health. It can also lead you to substantial financial losses, unhealthy relationships, and compromised safety. Addiction, contaminated behaviour, and many other unwholesome issues are possible outcomes if you compromise self-care. It is crucial to differentiate between smaller and broader issues. That is how you can make appropriate decisions about when to be flexible and when to stand firm in protecting your overall well-being.

Self-care includes your physical and mental health, dreams, desires, emotional and spiritual well-being, financial stability, career, relationships, and the management of stress and anxiety.

Once you recognize the importance of self-care, you can lead to transform your gray areas into golden opportunities more rapidly.

## Self-Affirmations

I am ............................ and I am able to face any form of manipulation. I honour my individuality and avoid changing without valid reasons. I stay true to who I am. I choose not to compromise my priorities for the sake of others' expectations. Self-love is my foundation and self-care is my daily ritual. Self-love and self-care creates a peace in my life. I embrace my right to self-care. I protect myself from manipulation, unnecessary changes, and unworthy compromises.

*"Self-care is how you take your power back." - Lalah Delia*

# Flow in Flow State

*"Flow is the peak performance state where you feel your best and you perform your best." - Steven Kotler*

Work is a big part of our lives. Different people have different experiences with it. Some like to work, some don't. Some are happy with work, some are not. People work at different speeds, some are very fast and some are slow. Some do focused work, some don't. There are also differences in the quality and quantity of work. Our main goal is to do more work in less time without compromising its quality. But only a few manage to have the capability. Everyone works, but only a few reach the desired success.

There may be many ways to work. One of them is the way of 'flow state.' Let's talk about this important technique. We have all experienced this flow state of our brain and body at some point in our lives. While working in a flow state, we felt like we did more work than we thought we could. The results of working in a flow state are excellent. It feels satisfying working in a flow state. We get the best outcome of quality and quantity of our work. At that time, working in flow state makes you your best version. All that happens because you choose the way of the flow state. I hope you understand the importance of the flow state in your life.

The flow state is when our brain and body work smoothly without any struggle. We become super alert and active. Our senses are extra active. It's like we are fully into what we are doing. Our focus is at its best and time seems to pass so quickly. We feel a special kind of joy while working in a flow state. This hyperactive state of the brain and body can last for about half an hour to a couple of hours.

Everyone can access the flow state in their work. Only a few are aware of it because using the flow state is a skill. One who is a master of this skill can apply it whenever and wherever they want. Here are some tricks to use to become a master of this skill.

- Consciousness supports reaching the flow state. A developed mind holds you back. Work on your consciousness.

- Free your thoughts to think clearly.

- This state requires a high focus. Keep away all the things that can distract you.

- Build a peaceful environment for working. It will be more beneficial if you choose to be close to nature.

- Have a clear vision of what you want and what you are doing. Don't be confused about your target.

- You must develop an interest in what you are doing. When you don't love what you are doing, you cannot fully engage in your work to reach the flow state.

- You can challenge yourself to do better than you did before. This will bring excitement that helps reach the flow state.

- You can use meditation and yoga to increase your concentration and focus.

- Enjoy what you do while using the flow state. It will be a motivation to use it again and again. You can remember the last experience of working in a flow state.

- Try to do any task in the flow state when you remember to use it.

There are many other benefits you can get from using the flow state. Here, I will mention why you must use the flow state.

- It's essential for your stable happiness.

- You gain work satisfaction as you are completely involved in it.

- You feel fresh as all your senses work together with hyper-activeness.

- You live in the present moment with full consciousness.

- It is good for your physical well-being. You will get best results in sports and other physical activities as it is the best coordination state of the brain and body.

- If you use the flow state, it will improve both quality and quantity of work.
- You must use this way in the 21st century. It makes you powerful enough to face this world full of competition.
- It enables you to be at the top.
- It helps you learn new skills faster.
- It will strengthen your willpower muscles.

## Self-Affirmations

I am……………………………….. and I embrace the flow state in my work, studies, and every activity. In this state, I unlock my full potential. The flow state is my key to a successful and happy life. I live in the present moment with full consciousness to apply the flow state. The flow state improves both the quality and quantity of my work. In the 21st century, I recognize the importance of the flow state. It helps me in a world full of competition and uncertainty.

*"Flow is the dance between your abilities and the challenges you face." - Amanda Harrison*

# Break Rigidity

*"The oak fought the wind and was broken, the willow bent when it must and survived."* - Robert Jordan

The simple meaning of rigidity is the state of being stiff, fixed, and impossible to bend. The opposite of rigidity is flexibility. Sometimes, when a situation demands your physical reaction, you may feel unable to move your bodies in the desired way. Other times, when you need to think and find a solution or answer, your brain does not respond properly. In both situations, you feel frozen and unable to use your brain and body according to what is required. At that point, you may feel like your brain and body are not under your control. This immovability of the brain and body is called rigidity. This is a common but severe problem in the current generation.

Mental rigidity happens when you strongly believe that what you know is the only truth. You feel resistant against considering other possibilities. From early on, you form fixed beliefs, attitudes, and ways of thinking. If you are not open to new ideas, then your brains become rigid. This can be harmful because it closes all the possibilities. You can't learn about fresh knowledge and new ways of dealing with everyday situations. Being flexible in your thinking helps you stay open to learning and adapting.

The 21st century is a century of uncertainty. Everything is changing. New challenges demand new solutions. Mental rigidity makes a person more vulnerable to the challenges of the 21st century. With mental rigidity, it is like passing through a dark night. For a rigid person, it becomes impossible to face all the challenges skilfully. Here, I will introduce you some "Gray to Gold" ways to break free from mental rigidity.

Knowledge is a core component of life. Always be ready to learn and update your knowledge. Check and replace old beliefs with the latest.

Avoid being egoistic. Ego is the enemy of knowledge and learning. Never consider yourself to have sufficient knowledge. You should always be hungry for learning. Be humble and allow knowledge to reach you effortlessly.

Be conscious and aware to prevent your mind from blocking your brain and body. A developed mind can create hurdles for the brain in finding solutions.

Recognize fixed patterns in your brain's functioning. Break them by going against and replacing them with desired patterns.

Avoid a fixed daily routine. Be creative and flexible in your life. Practice desired patterns for perfection.

Play chess to sharpen your brain by anticipating opponents' moves. This will develop planning and strategizing skills in you.

Participate in activities that require mental alertness. You can engage in crossword puzzles, memory card games, Sudoku, and vocabulary learning. These activities are the panaceas to mitigate mental rigidity.

Positive affirmations also help in the healing process of the brain. Positive affirmations have enough potential to break your rigid beliefs and free you from mental rigidity.

Meditation and yoga also contribute to the healing of the brain and makes it rigidity-proof.

Now, let's discuss body rigidity. Here the core component is laziness. Laziness is the state in which we don't want to engage in a particular activity. In this state, a person feels a lack of motivation and energy. They feel exhausted all the time. It feels to them that there are no logical benefits in participating in a specific task. It is important not to confuse laziness with procrastination. Procrastination is the wilful delay of a particular task. When a person decides to do something and suddenly changes the plan and delays it, they are procrastinating. This can be seen as the flexibility of the plan. But laziness should be considered as the rigidity of the body. The following are some causes of body rigidity.

1. Lack of willpower. A person with low willpower may not want to change their present state. That leads to laziness.

2. Lack of motivation and inspiration are also reasons behind body rigidity.

3. Any physical illness could also lead to inactivity of the body.

4. Obesity is one of the main causes of laziness or inactivity.

5. Lack of interest in physical or sports activities could also lead to body rigidity.

6. If the coordination between the brain and body is not up to the mark, it could lead to a rigid body.

7. When the brain sends messages to the body to act in particular circumstances, a developed mind can manipulate these messages and cause inactivity in the body.

8. The body is made of muscles. Muscles contract and relax to move the body. If someone is not doing physical activities, their muscles could get weak and rigid. They feel less strength in their body. This weakness of the body promotes laziness.

Now, we have discussed sufficiently on inactivity, laziness, or body rigidity. Let's proceed to "Gray to Gold" ways to break this rigidity and maximize the use of the body. These are the points that help you to keep your body in a healthy and active state.

1. Engage in various types of physical activities. It can include running, swimming, trekking, mountain climbing, and dancing. These activities will create a balanced state for your body.

2. Perform regular physical exercises to keep your body fit and active all the time.

3. Practice yoga, as it offers a variety of activities that make the body more flexible.

4. If you want to act in a particular way in a specific situation, practice that move repeatedly and create muscle memory.

5. Participate in sports activities. Sports combine fun with fitness.

6. Learn new skills that involve physical activities.

7. Do household work yourself. It involves physical activities that will gradually enhance your stamina.

8. Lose extra weight and free your body from this unwanted burden.

9. Be an efficient user of your energy. Use your energy for something worthwhile.

10. Practice is the key to making your moves more powerful and accurate. Train your muscles to memorize your desired moves. You can overpower body rigidity only through hard work and practice.

11. Most important part is to remember that laziness could occur because of malnutrition. If your body lacks specific nutrients, it will not act properly. Have healthy foods to avoid malnutrition.

## Self-Affirmations

I am ................................. and I am flexible in my thoughts and actions. I break free from rigidity. I open myself to new possibilities. My body is a powerhouse of strength and agility. I nurture it with physical and mental activities. I am the master of my brain and body. I protect my brain and body from the shackles of rigidity. When I sense rigidity, I take immediate steps to bring flexibility and openness. I put effort into keeping my mind and body active and flexible all the time.

*"Rigidity leads to weakness; flexibility leads to strength."*
*- Tony Robbins*

# Reaction Rules

*"Life is 10% what happens to us and 90% how we react to it."*
*- Charles R. Swindoll*

Every action has reaction. It is not only a rule of physics but also of nature. Without action, there is no reaction. Sometimes a reaction itself becomes an action for another reaction. It is possible that an action is not followed by a reaction. It is important to note that no reaction is itself a reaction. In this chapter, I am addressing the actions and reactions of us, humans. We will discuss how we act and react. It is an important part of behaviour so that we must learn about the actions and reactions we encounter in daily life. Sometimes it becomes hard to differentiate between an action and a reaction. In such situations, the reactions of others seem like their actions. A person always considers his actions as reactions to something. No one knows or accepts who initiated it all with their action. Thus, the action and reaction game begins and continues.

Reaction is a valuable tool if we use it efficiently. A reaction could also be a self-harming weapon if we deal with carelessness. It has the potential to make us strong or weak. The role of reaction in life cannot be ignored. It is crucial to understand and use it skilfully. It becomes more important in the era of over competition. The 21st century is the time where survival demands refined actions and reactions. There is no scope for miscalculation of actions and reactions. Here, we will discuss three "Gray to Gold" rules for actions and reactions. If you follow these rules, it will bring you good things. It will protect you from adverse outcomes of your behaviour. These rules are different from each other and you must use them for specific purposes. The ability to analyze circumstances will help you in choosing the best option. Here are the rules.....

## Be indifferent

Every time something is happening around you, it is impossible to react to everything. And if you try to do so, it is foolish. Every reaction is a loss of energy. A reactions like money; it should be used wisely. If something doesn't deserve your reaction, why waste it? No reaction is also a reaction. Just be calm and composed, observe and analyze the situation, then decide what to do. If anything occurs suddenly, pause, breathe, and give yourself enough time to react. Always remember that you have the option of no reaction.

## Don't be impulsive

Sometimes a particular situation occurs and you feel a strong urge to react. If it's done frequently, then this urge to react becomes a hidden habit. In this condition, you may struggle to decide how to react properly. Any manipulator can take advantage of your habitual reactions. Your reactions to something should be controlled and appropriate for the situation. The intensity of energy should match the requirement. When you are playing the game, you must create a balance between action and reaction. You must have focus, energy, and interest to achieve this balance. Mindfulness and emotional intelligence are also important tools for dealing with such situations.

## Be the boss of your reactions

Don't let your reactions cause loss for you. Use your reactions to your advantage. Uncontrolled reactions are like wild animals and can put you in danger at any time. Controlled reactions are like pet animals and always provide you something positive. Be the master of your reactions. Practice your reactions before applying them. Be skilled in using reactions. Learn from the experiences of your past reactions. You can also learn by observing others' reactions.

Everything you achieve is because of how you react. Same when you lose something, it's because of you made wrong choices in how you reacted. Your responses or reactions will shape the path you will walk. If you want to get success, it is important to have the right and appropriate actions and reactions. On the other hand, if you don't react wisely, it can lead you to failures and hard times. Now I hope you understand that actions and reactions hold immense power. It helps you to give direction to your journey. Once you become a master of this art, you can create your story where successes are celebrated, and mistakes become opportunities to learn and grow.

## Self-Affirmations

I am........................................ and I am in control of my actions and reactions. My responses are a reflection of my strength and self-control. I choose mindful reactions that lead to positive outcomes. No external force can manipulate my reactions without my will. I embrace challenges with calmness and consciousness. I ignore reactions that don't contribute to my well-being. I learn and grow from every experience to be skilled in using better reactions.

*"It's not what happens to you, but how you react to it that matters." - Epictetus*

# Right Here and Right Now

*"The present moment is the only moment available to us, and it is the door to all moments." - Thich Nhat Hanh*

"Here and now" is a magical phrase. It signifies that everything exists in the present. The present is the playground of any actions. The past and future are beyond our limits. Maintaining order in everything is essential for a better life and this could be achieved through working in the present. Living in the present leaves no pendency of work and life flows smoothly.

Another advantage of embracing the way of being "Here and Now" is that it keeps you free from the mind. The mind, in Hindi is 'Manh', a state where we lose control of self and the cloud of negative thoughts, feelings, and emotions overpower our brain and body. You are not your mind; your brain is not your mind. The state of working with higher focus is only achievable by being in the present. "Here and Now" functions as a powerful tool that offers so many psychological benefits. The brain is the most important organ in our body. To ensure a healthy brain, it must be free from anxiety and depression. Addiction to dopamine hormone by instant pleasure as well as cortisol hormone by anxiety and sadness also damages the efficiency of the brain. The brain suffers when it is burdened with excessive thoughts or over thinking. These negative and excessive thoughts release toxic hormones and elements in our brain and body.

Here, I am going to make clear the distinction between the mind and the brain. The brain is a vital organ and controls almost every function of the body. On the other hand, the mind carries a negative image. The mind is nothing but a collection or cloud of negative thoughts intermingled with negative feelings and emotions. The mind is in a non-physical state. When the mind develops within our brain, it creates a detrimental impact on the brain and body. Simply, excessive negative thoughts can negatively impact the functioning of the brain. This directly affects our body and overall life. That is why it becomes crucial to free our brain from the grip of the mind.

Individuals are addicted to over thinking. They think it leads to great solutions but could not succeed. Instead, they develop the habit of over thinking by repeating it. Our senses like vision, hearing, touch, smell, taste and the inner instinct connect us with the environment. They are all ultimately related to the brain. When the mind takes control, the first thing it damages is our sensory awareness. It causes detachment from our surroundings. In this state, we remain inactive toward the events happening around us. The mind has enough potential to destroy our lives and those of others. For example, a person riding a bike at full speed in a crowded area. If he gets trapped in over thinking, he may miss crucial details and that can lead to an unfortunate accident.

The habit of over thinking inculcates laziness in a person which is the root cause of his suffering. Laziness arises when our senses do not support our brain and body. It causes a habit of procrastination. Developed mind depletes energy from both the brain and body. It makes it challenging to gather the required energy or willpower to do a task. Constant over thinking drains all the willpower and confidence.

Being Here and Now with active senses empowers us to effortlessly complete any task. It increases confidence and strengthens willpower because we get satisfaction of completing tasks. When the mind develops, it distracts us from the current task and suggests other options for instant gratification. It challenges the worthiness of the current task. It throws temptations, cravings, and excuses for leaving the present task. This is how the mind damages our harmony with work. It also decreases our interest in the work and lures us toward pleasure. Work is considered as a form of worship. It rewards those who approach it with a high level of attention, focus, devotion, and interest. If you embrace "Here and Now" it will ensure undisturbed focus on your present task.

Let us try to crack it with an example, suppose you are sitting with person 'A' and thinking about 'B', and when sitting with person 'B' and thinking about "A'. This is an injustice to both. True justice occurs when you fully engage with 'A' when you are with them and similarly with 'B'. It strengthens your good relations with both. The same thing happens with any activity you do.

We all know the importance of gratitude. Being Here and Now enables us to recognize even small assistance and allows us to express gratitude at the same time. Being Here and Now is very important for gratitude to work in your favour.

In the chapter on the flow state concept, I will illustrate how the "Here and Now" helps to reach the most effective way of doing any task. This concept is very easy to understand but its application requires habitual practice. Creating good habits, a topic for later discussion, requires repetition, that is only possible by being in the present moment. Therefore, you must stay in the present moment to get plenty of benefits.

## Self-Affirmations

I am………………………………….. and I am fully present in every moment and it allows me to fully engage with my life. I release worries about the past and future. I focus on what I can do now. Each breath I take connects me to the present reality. I appreciate the beauty of the present moment and find joy in it. I let go of all the distractions created by the mind. The present is a gift and I enjoy every moment of it. I embrace the present with immense gratitude.

*"Forever is composed of nows." - Emily Dickinson*

# Living with Less

*"The more you have, the more you are occupied. The less you have, the more free you are."* - Mother Teresa

After the industrial revolution, the world faced a flood of new products for the first time. People once lived with only essential items for their survival, and they were leading simple lives based on only basic needs. Only the powerful and the richest men enjoyed luxuries, the rest of the people maintained a very simple lifestyle. At that time, the common man was working only for survival. After the Industrial Revolution, there was a surplus of new products, and common people were lured by advertisements to use more new products. Innocent public worked more hours to afford the new products. First, it began as an option to buy these products, but with time, it became habitual. Thus, people were trapped in the vicious cycle of habitual continuous consumption.

People were too busy with various social activities and entertainment to understand this shift. The Industrial Revolution's impact was global, and that led to wars fuelled by greed for wealth and power. These wars resulted in significant human suffering that was never done before. Here, my aim is to show you the power of industries and their strategies and their impact on the common man. Industries are there for profit. They use various methods to exploit common people for their financial gain. They use advertisements to create desires to buy product after turning that into a necessity. They use professionals to create psychological methods in advertisements to indirectly force consumers to buy their products.

If we talk about today, the availability of online shopping further increases this addiction with notifications and personalized suggestions. The instant gratification and release of dopamine become a new addiction that makes users purchase unnecessary items. That all leads to filling the house with unnecessary items. Each product has a stimulus power that demands customers' attention.

A house with so much stuff divides the attention of a person. Unfocused mind consume more willpower for work which requires more focus. Possibly with low willpower we can leave task unfinished. One major mistake we are making is that we value a product in monetary terms. The real cost includes other essential aspects of our life. For example, a teenager demands an expensive tablet after being manipulated by an advertisement. The cost he will pay is not only money, it also includes other aspects of his life like – it affects his relationship with his parents, his overall happiness, his self-respect, health, and valuable time. His mistake is not that he insisted on his parents buying that for him. Instead, he was manipulated by that advertisement. It becomes important to learn about the advertising industry and its manipulative behaviour.

The only solution lies in adopting a way of 'living with less'. This way simplifies life and emphasizes focusing on only essential and meaningful possessions. This way it allows a person to work with concentration. Scientifically, it's proven that our brain and body become strong in scarcity. Those who lived with less are physically strong and mentally sound. They find it easy to deal with harsh conditions and challenges.

This way also contributes to social welfare by inspiring others to be minimalist. For example, a culture of excessive consumption creates unhealthy competition in the society. This excessive consumption leads to environmental pollution. You can show gratitude to Mother Earth and society by minimizing plastic waste and unnecessary competition for consumption. Over-dependence on gadgets weakens people and negatively impacts their ability to help themselves and others. On the other hand, those who are following the way of 'living with less' can face challenges and survive with minimal resources.

The Zen sect of Buddhism supports the way of 'living with less.' The Monks living in monasteries, strictly follow a lifestyle with minimal possessions. They believe in simplicity for internal peace and maintaining overall health through exposure to extreme conditions.

In conclusion, I want to reiterate the old saying, 'simple living is happy living'. If you choose the way to 'live with less', you are going to have a fulfilling and happy life.

## Self-Affirmations

I am ………………………………….. and I embrace simplicity. I find joy in owning only what is truly important in my life. My happiness is not defined by material possessions. I release the need for excess in my life. I am free from the burden and understand that true wealth lies in contentment and gratitude. I prioritize experiences over possessions. I let go of unnecessary belongings to liberate myself. I show my gratitude to nature by choosing a minimalist lifestyle. I celebrate the freedom that comes with my minimalist lifestyle.

*"It is preoccupation with possessions, more than anything else, that prevents us from living freely and nobly." - Bertrand Russell*

# Happy Parents Are the Best Parents

*"Parents can only give good advice or put them on the right paths, but the final forming of a person's character lies in their own hands." - Anne Frank*

It is hard to win the hearts of parents. All parents are hard to please with their children's actions. It is challenging to make your parents happy. If you succeed in winning their hearts, it means you have conquered half the world. Satisfied and happy parents are the biggest supporters. Unhappy ones can create significant hindrances in the holistic development of their children. Parents play an important role in shaping our lives. Only some parents possess the skill to raise brilliant kids, others may not. Almost all parents love their children, except those with narcissistic personalities. We receive a large part of love and affection from our parents. We can experience the purest form of unconditional love only from them. We need to be grateful to them. Raising a child is a hard task as parents have to face everyday challenges.

After a child reaches 10-12 years of age, a cold war might start between them and their parents. Parents make decisions that may or may not suit children. Disagreements on any decisions can lead to small conflicts. Thus, it becomes very important for kids to understand the art of conflict management with their parents. And the good thing is that it is a simple skill to learn because it follows fixed rules and principles.

## Arguments are always futile.

Arguments leads nowhere. It should be avoided both by parents and children. No one listens to either advice or explanations in a louder voice. No arguments reach a conclusion and all attempts for this go in vain. The only thing we get from arguments is hatred for each other. Ego or self-respect is precious for every person, and everyone wants to defend it. In arguments, we directly hit the ego of the next person. From now on, an ego-hurt person will never love or respect you. Also, in his mind, resentment grows and that could last for a long time. If it is not repaired well in time, it may lead to undesired consequences. Arguments are the worst form of communication. No one wins an argument.

## Respect your parents.

Your parents suffer a lot when they are raising you. They deserve your respect. If you respect your parents, you will never have a scarcity of love and affection from them. That love and affection provide a base for a happy life for you. Without love and affection, dissatisfaction will develop inside you and your happiness will disappear. What you give is what you will get. If you respect your parents, they will listen to you and you can explain what you want.

## Have a talk.

Each day we have to make decisions. If you need to make any decisions on something of significant importance, just go and discuss it with your parents. This improves trust between you and your parents. You can also resolve any past trust issues with sincere discussions. Making decisions without involving your parents creates a gap between you and your parents.

## Don't lie to them.

Lying is the main cause of trust issues. If you deceive someone his trust will disappear. Your parents are adept at catching your lies. They know you deeply because you grew up in front of your parents. They are aware of your strengths, weaknesses, capabilities, and gray areas. Trying to fool them is futile. Parents prefer honesty from you. Once you are caught lying, rebuilding parental trust will be hard for you. It leads them to emotional pain. Suspicion from parents will hurt you. Their inquiries will fill you with resentment. If they are getting information about you from any external source, it can disrupt the peace at home. All this chaos can be avoided by embracing a simple way and that is, "Don't lie to your parents."

## Show them you are mature.

Every parent wishes for their kids to be mature. They examine your maturity through observations of your behaviour and actions. Try to impress your parents by treating them and others with kindness. Enhance your communication skills and assist your parents in their daily struggles. Take responsibility for your actions and show confidence in your efforts. Show them that you are capable through your actions, not by words. Take care of your grandparents and siblings. Your parents will undoubtedly perceive your these qualities and consider you as a mature person. Once you succeed in recognizing your maturity, your parents will be more open to consider your suggestions and decisions.

## Use a sense of humour

Handling any relationship is challenging. So many factors require attention for a healthy relationship. In this fast-paced world, it becomes difficult to maintain personal and social life together. Unfulfilled expectations of parents can lead to bitterness. Misunderstandings with parents are not uncommon. A sense of humour can lighten a tense environment. Humour possesses the power to resolve conflict and refresh relationships. It is a superior remedy for healing broken relationships.

## Make your scorecard healthy

Comparison is inherent in human nature, and parents are no exception. They may compare you with the children of their friends, relatives, or neighbours. Your scorecard isa fundamental parameter for others to evaluate you. Make an effort to achieve good scores to prevent sadness for your parents. Also, to some extent, your scorecard influences how your decisions will be perceived by your parents. Believe me, scoring well is not a difficult task and the rewards will be incredibly sweet.

## Never compare your parents with others

Parents put in so much effort to raise a child. They face countless struggles to provide you with a comfortable life. You are the most significant part of your parents' lives. No one on earth can give you more affection, love, and care than your parents. When you compare your parents with others, it hurts them and makes them feel humiliated. It destroys their sense of importance in your life. Always recognize their importance in your life.

## Have a sincere company

Our company reflects our class. It's psychologically proven that a large part of our personality is shaped by our friends. Your parents are aware of this fact. They always observe your company and your friends. If your friends are not sincere, then parents will impose restrictions on you that you may not like. If your company is sincere, then parents will feel at ease and you will be able to enjoy your freedom.

## Have good habits

Every parent appreciates good habits and dislikes the bad habits of their children. It is not acceptable to parents that you have a few good habits and more bad habits. Don't try to justify yourself based on a few good habits, it will not be sufficient. Increase your good habits and you will be liked by your parents.

## Obey family rules

Every system operates on rules and regulations, and a family function similarly. Each family is unique and has its own set of rules and regulations. Comparing two families can be a ridiculous idea. Our parents establish rules to ensure the smooth running of the family. They expect from us thatwe will cooperate and assist them. When you break the rules, it hurts your parents. Make the habit of supporting the general rules of the family.

## Self-Affirmations

I am …………………………………………….. and I deeply respect and honour my parents for the love and sacrifices they have made for me. I choose to obey my parents with respect. I recognize the importance of them in my life. I use humour with my parents as it lightens the atmosphere and strengthens my bond with them. I am surrounded by friends with whom my parents feel comfortable. My relationship with my parents is based on trust, love, and open communication. I am grateful for the harmonious and respectful environment of my family.

> *"Parents were the only ones obligated to love you; from the rest of the world, you had to earn it." - Ann Brashares*

# Break Free from Addiction

*"The chains of addiction are too weak to be felt until they are too strong to be broken." - Samuel Johnson*

The toughest struggle a person faces in addiction is the internal battle with himself. Addiction acts like a shadow. It is an unwelcome companion of one's life journey. It begins with harmless curiosity, but over time it transforms into a powerful obstacle that is difficult to get rid of. The addiction leaves that person with scars, among them some are visible, and others hidden. In the end, it becomes a challenging task to overcome.

Addiction holds enough power to shape someone's life. It brings him down and stop him from reaching his full potential. It consistently has a negative impact. It ruins lives. It prevents individuals from moving toward a bright future. This cycle of addiction leads to emotional vulnerability. It depletes all joy and happiness. It replaces them with stress, anxiety and depression. With his diminished self-confidence, a person with addiction begins to doubt his capabilities. When his earning capacity is badly affected, it leads him to poor financial choices. The cost of addiction is not just monetary. It has psychological, emotional, and physical after-effects. Those caught in the grip of addiction can become a source of problems for their loved ones.

As the effects of addiction weaken after some time and the person comes back into normal life, it fills him with guilt, shame and self-pity. During this period, he has a strong desire to bid farewell to the unwanted companion. He tries hard and makes promises to himself and others. He forms resolutions and spends his limited willpower. Despite these efforts, he finds himself overpowered by the cravings and temptations. His self-control slips away. His promises and resolutions weaken and addiction reclaims its position. This vicious circle continues. This all illustrates how addiction ruins what was once a beautiful life.

People often find themselves confused about addiction. They struggle to distinguish it from other activities. Many addictive behaviours or actions are mistakenly perceived as normal. Numerous addictive substances have become integral parts of social rituals deeply intertwined with culture. Adolescents have no awareness about addiction. It is challenging for them to differentiate between addictive and normal activities. Therefore, I would like to clarify various types of addiction so that you can identify any addictive activity.

There are many addictions prevalent in society. Here are some to mention…

Drinking alcohol, smoking, chewing tobacco, and intake of drugs through sniffing, smelling, injecting, and swallowing are substance-based addictions.

Watching porn, frequent masturbation, uncontrolled desires for sex, and other abnormal sexual behaviours are considered sexual addictions.

Some individuals are addicted to behaving in specific patterns. They feel unable to resist certain actions even when they are aware of the consequences. This behavioural addiction may involve anger, hatred, violence, greediness, and unreasonable fear. People with these abnormalities are often labelled as eccentric in society.

When a person is habitual of a particular emotion. This specific emotion continuously generates a satisfactory experience. When done frequently, it becomes an emotional addiction. Emotions are formed in the brain through the release of certain chemicals. Individuals with emotional addiction seek the frequent release of these chemicals. And this is how they become emotionally addicted.

In the 21st century, almost everyone has a screen in their pocket. This is a phenomenon unprecedented in human history. This digital world helps us in dealing with various daily situations. At the same time, it is creating dependency. Data reveals that an individual's screen time is increasing day by day. It indicates growing digital addiction in the current generation.

Craving food, shopping excessively, and engaging in a normal activity abnormally are also considered addictions.

The general psychology behind addiction revolves around four keywords: stimulus, action, pleasure, and repetition. When a person encounters any stimulus, they act in a certain pattern. In return, he experiences pleasure or reward and then repeat the cycle for more pleasure. This cycle creates addiction. This cycle can transform a normal person into someone abnormal by introducing addiction in their life.

I think we have discussed enough about addiction and the problems it creates. Now is the time to explore solutions. There are mainly two types of solutions: preventive solutions and curative solutions. Let's discuss both one by one.

There is a popular saying that prevention is better than cure. Prevention is a powerful tool to deal with unfavourable happenings. Unfortunately, its importance is not recognized. Here, I am going to suggest you with some addiction prevention ways worth following:

You must make it a habit to control your curiosity of exploring unworthy things. Learn about the harmful aspects of any activity through observation rather than personal experience. Stay away from addiction and observe it from a distance.

If you suspect any activity is an addiction, go to authentic sources and confirm it. Identifying addiction is a crucial preventive measure.

Do not accept any type of addictive offerings. Generally, a person lacks the courage to start an addiction on their own. It is someone else who offers and influences to do it. Clearly and strongly say no to any addictive offerings.

There is no need to believe in rituals that promote addiction in any way. You must be doubtful and avoid engagement with practices that encourage addictive behaviours.

The most important factor is your company. You must avoid having friends with any type of addiction. If your friend is engaged in such behaviour, encourage them to leave the addiction or distance yourself from them.

If one is stuck in the vicious circle of addiction, they can still recover and lead a normal life. It requires willpower, self-control, emotional support, dedication, and discipline on the journey out of any addiction. Here I will discuss some curative ways to overcome addiction.

After identifying addiction, gather willpower and self-confidence. Create a proper plan. Discipline will play a vital role, so don't ignore it. You must avoid breaking resolutions because this drains your willpower.

Immediately distance yourself from people, places, and other things related to addiction. Do not give them a second chance to ruin your beautiful life.

It takes 66 days to clear the mind from addiction. After 66 days of a strict and disciplined routine, there will be no remnants of addiction to bother you in your brain.

Do not be alone. Loneliness often welcomes addiction cravings. Try to be with someone. Each morning prepare your routine with vibrant and good people to create a positive and supportive environment around you.

Do not sit idle; instead, keep yourself busy. Remember the famous saying, "An idle mind is the devil's workshop." Engage in work and find something to do. Be an active worker. Staying busy will help keep cravings and addiction away.

Here, your physical fitness goals can play a very productive and vital role. Put your focus on your fitness. It will inspire and motivate you. It strengthens your willpower and gives you enough confidence to fight this battle with addiction.

You can also seek help from medical experts. There is no need to be shy or feel ashamed. Doctors are considered gods and gods are never going to judge you. They are there to help you.

Find your interests, favourite sports, and hobbies. You should channel your energy into something productive. This is where you can transform your challenges into opportunities and turn the gray areas of your life into gold.

You can read good literature or nonfiction books to heal yourself. Additionally, you can join yoga or meditation to regain self-control with physical and mental health.

## Self-Affirmations

I am ………………………………….. and my strength is greater than any addictive substance. I recognize the importance of a healthier lifestyle. I always care for the health of my brain and body. I use technology mindfully. I set boundaries to prevent digital screen addiction. I always prioritize real-world experiences. My time away from screens is an investment in my overall well-being. I am conscious of my habits. I am aware of harmful behavioural patterns. I nourish my body with healthy foods and my brain with good thoughts. I embrace self-care to heal myself.

> *"Addiction is the only prison where the locks are on the inside." – Unknown*

# Worship your Work

*"Far and away the best prize that life has to offer is the chance to work hard at work worth doing." - Theodore Roosevelt*

My father's favourite words are, "There is no important person but work is important; a person is never worshipped, but his work is worshipped." God gives us life to work, a body to work, a brain to work, opportunities to work, challenges to work, hardships to work, problems to work, failures to work, hope to work, strength to work, motivation to work, inspiration to work, days to work, weather to work, natural calamities to work, and the series never end. It simply means that God wants us to work.

Each of us has our own goals and dreams in life. We want to achieve something or get something to establish ourselves in society. The only thing we need is to work. Through appropriate work, we can achieve whatever we want. Let's learn with an example. Consider two friends, A and B. First, let's see what A is doing. A is the son of rich parents who provide him with everything he needs. With all the luxury, he spends his days having fun. He depends on assistants for everything. With time, he loses interest in every aspect of life. His satisfaction with life decreases and that leads him to unhappiness. As he doesn't have much skills and the willpower to do something specific. He earns no respect from family and friends and at last, he loses self-respect and self-belief. Low confidence and low self-esteem push him toward addiction and violence that could lead to even worse. One day he asks God, "What was my mistake?" God replies, "You did not choose the way to work."

Now, let's look at B. He was born into a middle-class family. His father works in the government sector on a salary basis. His father can only provide basic needs. In the beginning, B insists on more but changes his mind after understanding the family's actual condition. He helps his mother, grandparents, and father. At school, he aids teachers in maintaining discipline. He is also always ready to help friends. He finds pleasure in working on his farm with nature. He studies hard and understands his talents which leads him to achieve his desired targets and make family and friends proud. He pursues social welfare. He leads a successful and meaningful life. One day, he asks God "Why are you so benevolent with me?", and God replies, "My son, you chose the way to work."

These stories emphasize the importance of work. Work itself plays the role of a merciful God; work is God. It is work that creates our identity, strengthens relationships, earns money to spend, and also provides access to essential goods and services. Active work engages all the senses and brings us into the present moment. Active work always surpasses passive work. Awareness of our actions allows full control over them.

There is no high or low work, each work deserves respect. Every individual is assigned their role in a system which contributes to its functioning. Coordination and team spirit enhance the outcomes of the system. Before going into any work, you must always consider work questions like what, when, how, where, how much, when to stop, when to abstain, with whom, what to use, and possible side effects. When you get all the answers, then only you should proceed to work.

Throughout your life, you will experience people talking about hard work and easy work. The distinction lies only in planning, motivation, willpower and energy. There is no hard work; instead, our mindset makes it so. If you are doing a specific work, with time and practice, it will be easy for you to do it. If you have answers to essential work questions, confidence, willpower, practice and energy, any work will be easy and interesting for you.

On Earth, we are 8 billion people and we all are different from one another. These differences arise from work choices based on the "Karma Rule." The common man is confused by the complex social fabric and the uncertainty of the 21st century. It requires smartness and self-awareness to find appropriate work. If you understand the importance of the work questions mentioned above, you will find no difficulty in finding the best opportunities to work. If you apply these work questions daily, you will be a master in differentiating between right and wrong.

In conclusion, I strongly advise you to embrace the concept "Be a worker, worship your work, be an aware worker, get your work answers before working, and create a habit of working."

## Self-Affirmations

I am............................................. and I am a dedicated worker. My work is an expression of my talents and abilities. I choose work to grow, learn, and create value in my life. Before starting any work, I clear my mind by asking work questions like why, what, where, when, who, how much, and how long. I strongly believe that my work is a journey of self-discovery. I ensure the best strategic approach to work. I value my time and energy and direct them toward my desired work. I am the architect of my life, and I shape it by choosing the way to work. I am grateful to God as He gave me a lot of work to do.

> *"Your work is going to fill a large part of your life, and the only way to be truly satisfied is to do what you believe is great work." - Steve Jobs*

# Say No to Vultures

*"Saying 'no' is a big, delicious step toward freedom."*
*- Glennon Doyle*

There are so many vultures around you. Each one has their own expectations of you. Everyone wants to mold your lives to fit their needs. They try to use you as much as possible. They set rules for you to follow and create psychological structures to ensure you behave accordingly. They use dark psychology tricks like ignoring, appreciating, and making you feel great. They create thoughts, feelings, and emotions in you so that you obey them. They set examples and take advantage of your cravings and temptations. They trap you by exploiting your weaknesses to use your strengths. They can create an artificial atmosphere where your dreams and desires seem to be fulfilled, sometimes they do it themselves, and sometimes they hire professionals.

They create a fear of the future and promise to protect you from it. They also take advantage of your habits and fixed behavior patterns. They can create an obedient mindset. They can dull your senses. They hire us, pay us, train us, give incentives, and offer social security to use us.

Misinformation, narrative warfare, and propaganda are other ways to occupy your minds. Advertisements play a big role in shaping your desires. People also use your relationships with them. Sometimes they pressurize you for the favors they've done for you in the past. Sometimes you accept because you are attracted by confidence or the power they have. Charismatic personalities have enough aura to make you agree to their proposals. People flatter you and make you feel good until they get what they need from you. Everyone uses different techniques to deal with you.

Even your mind, filled with negative thoughts, emotions and feelings, is always ready to harm you. The mind is like a parasite and it harms its owner. It has so many ways to occupy your brain and body and then make decisions for you. The mind suggests negative things and offers you pleasure in the form of cravings and temptations. It keeps your senses deteriorated. In that condition, you do whatever the mind orders. Your 'yes' to the mind proves fatal to your well-being.

What these vultures want is simple yes from you. They want you to obey them, follow them, accept their decisions, and agree to their proposals. They want to use your life to change theirs. They want to take control of your life to ensure their freedom. They want to fulfill their desires and dreams by ruining yours. They want to secure their future by spoiling yours. They want you to work so they can rest. They want to use you to protect themselves from being used by others. All they need is your simple 'yeses'.

Habit and behavior pattern of saying 'yes' is not as simple as you think. It looks cool and positive to say yes, but this habit is not considered good when it comes to wisdom. Saying yes can lead you to severe circumstances. Saying yes opens all the options for vulnerability. Saying yes means giving control to someone else. After your yes, they will lead you wherever they want and anything could happen in between. After your yes, your resources could be exploited. You could not use your time however you want. Your dreams and desires mean nothing to anyone. If any big incident emerges from your yes, your future could be in danger. Your willpower and confidence could be drained by a simple yes. Your habit of saying yes can deteriorate your confidence as you cannot resist and say no. Your self-care and self-love could be badly affected. It's possible that your best friend, money, could get angry with you. Many aftereffects could occur as a result of saying yes.

Here I am not suggesting that it's bad to say yes and good to say no all the time. My intention is to make you aware of your habit of saying yes. Your habit plays a vital role. It's okay to say yes when the situation is ordinary. It's okay to say yes when it causes no harm to you. For a good purpose, it is okay to say yes. When your priorities, time, and safety are not compromised, it is okay to say yes.

Now, in what possible circumstances should you avoid saying yes? Here are some suggestions:

### Say yes to your instinct

Instinct is our inner voice. It is based on our previous experience and knowledge. You must be aware of this inner voice. Most of the time, it's right. When you are stuck between yes and no, observe what your instinct is suggesting. Once you believe you are right, never let others influence your decisions.

### Say no to an addictive offering

Many times, people around you may attract you toward addiction. Addiction spoils life. Stay away and say no to addiction.

### Say no to unwanted risk

Risks are part of life. But unwanted risk is dangerous because it involves carelessness. You must always avoid it.

### Say no to a fool

Always remember not to follow a fool. Fools are always ready to make mistakes or blunders without any reason. Keep a safe distance. Never accept a proposal offered by a fool. Here, a fool represents people with less knowledge but overconfidence.

### Never say yes to an overly emotional person

It's okay to be emotional but when a person is full of emotions, they cannot make the right decisions. They will regret that decision after the emotion fades. Never agree to do what an overly emotional person wants you to do.

### Say no when your priority is compromised

Your decisions should align with your priorities. A person who easily compromises their priorities cannot achieve what they desire. Always respect your priorities. When someone tries to influence you to compromise, say no. People respect those who respect their priorities.

## Say no to a fake person

Many people come and go in your lives. Some are natural and some are disguised. A fake person comes into our life to take something of their interest. They impress you with artificial gestures. They try to find your vulnerabilities. They take advantage and then run away. Say no when you identify a fake person.

## Say no to opportunist

Some people will always consider your resources and money more than you. They want to use your resources and promote you to spend more. When you find someone who has an evil eye on your money and resources, say no.

## Say no to manipulation

Some people are skilled manipulators. They use dark psychological tricks. When you find you are going to be manipulated, say no.

## Say a strong no to your cravings and temptations

Your mind is not your brain. It plays a lead role in spoiling a beautiful life. It offers pleasurable ideas and creates cravings and temptations. You feel it hard to say no to the mind because you can't distinguish between yourself and mind without practice. Reject what your mind offers in the form of cravings and temptations.

## Say no to bad habits

Bad habits have enough power to ruin your life. Always identify bad habits and say no to them. A simple no can protect your life from being ruined by toxic bad habits.

## Self-affirmations

I am..........................................and I confidently reject manipulators. I ensure my freedom by setting clear boundaries. I am strong enough to resist the temptations of any addiction. I refuse to engage with a person who is driven by selfish motives. I stand resolute against cravings by any bad habits. I always avoid fools and their decisions. I only nurture relationships based on trust and wisdom. I trust authentic people and distance myself from fake people. I reject the extravagance that can diminish my resources. I am free from bad habits because I know how to say no to them.

*"The difference between successful people and very successful people is that very successful people say 'no' to almost everything."*
*- Warren Buffett*

# Grow in Nature

*"Look deep into nature, and then you will understand everything better."* - Albert Einstein

The universe is immense and holds immense power. It encompasses everything that exists, and there is nothing beyond it. Everything happens within it. It is full of secrets, with only a few revealed. God is not hidden from us; the universe is God. Our planet Earth is a tiny part of the universe. As far as we know, only Earth has a life support system. We are discovering the secrets of the universe one by one. We feel that each chapter is filled with surprises beyond our imagination.

Nature is one of the gifts God has given to us. This gift itself is full of wonderful presents. Mother Nature has provided uncountable blessings to all of us without any discrimination. Nature has given us a life-supporting system that includes oceans, seas, rivers, mountains, deserts, plains, plateaus, valleys, atmosphere, rain, seasons, forests, animals, trees, fish, air, water, fruits, grains, ecosystems, our bodies, greenery, tranquillity, feelings, emotions, wisdom, and most importantly, life. Everything mentioned above is given to us. We are not entitled to them. We can try to claim any possessions and may succeed for a time. Ultimately nature reclaims what belongs to it. It includes our lives also.

Nature is the supreme power. It has powers beyond our imagination. It possesses both constructive and destructive forces. These forces balance positives and negatives to sustain life on Earth. Nature provides abundant resources for inhabitants. Nature has its rules and regulations to maintain the balance. It doesn't mean that nature interferes excessively. It grants us enough liberty in our choices to ensure our survival.

A person who follows the rules, regulations, and the system created by nature has nothing to worry about. A person who loves and respects Mother Nature will receive numerous blessings. They will be taken care of by Nature. Nature makes their survival easier. Those who go against nature will suffer. Nature eliminates those rebels in the end. Therefore, it is crucial to align with nature.

The main problem arises in understanding what nature wants from us. We are unaware about the rules and regulations of Nature. We have to learn about nature from the first day to the last breath of life. Everything we learn is about our nature. Nature holds numerous secrets to unveil one by one. Fortunately, nature has granted us the ability to store learned knowledge through languages. Nature allows us the transfer of knowledge to the next generation. Our ancestors passed on their knowledge about nature. We are using that knowledge in running the entire system. It is essential to note that what we have discovered is only a small part of nature. Many secrets are yet to be revealed. You can get the right and crucial knowledge by curiosity, observation, discussion, experiences, and practical engagement.

Our relationship with nature should be like our relationship with our mother. Being a true son of nature opens the door for Mother Nature to share blessings. If your relation is established with nature, you are blessed.

"How to be close to nature" is probably your next question. I suggest some "Gray to Gold "steps you can take toward nature.

Have respect and care for nature and its components. Do whatever is possible to conserve nature.

You can explore nature by visiting mountains, forests, rivers, lakes, waterfalls, gardens, and anywhere you find close to nature. Feel nature, appreciate its beauty and show affection toward it. Natural tourism is the best form of tourism.

Love animals. There are a variety of animals surrounding us. You should develop a brotherly relationship with them and avoid exploiting them. Show them kindness.

You can have affection toward greenery. Trees provide us with the oxygen we breathe. You should avoid preferring concrete forests over real ones. Hug a tree and observe how good you start feeling.

You can spend time with nature and make it a habit to do so frequently. Also, you can take a walk in nature and engage in physical exercise with the purest oxygen.

You can have a Zen garden in your office. The beauty of a Zen garden will fascinate and satisfy your soul.

You can create a small garden in your home. It could become a fulfilling hobby and will bring many more good things into your life.

You can have pet animals for a supply of unconditional love.

You can go to the terrace at night and gaze at the moon and stars. You can also engage in a conversation with them. Here, you can feel the warmth of the universe and nature.

You can open your arms, close your eyes, and feel the breeze. It will feel like nature is talking to you.

There are numerous benefits we are already receiving from nature. If you succeed in building a strong bond with nature, you will gain immense gifts from it. Here, I would like to mention some of the gifts we receive after getting close to nature.

It keeps us calm and composed. It provides a long-lasting inner peace.

It is beneficial for our physical, mental, and emotional well-being.

Nature brings us the true nature of happiness. Which is more original and stable than that obtained from other sources.

Spending time with nature helps us deal with anxiety and depression. It is like a panacea for healing mental illness.

Nature has immense power to heal us from many diseases.

Nature is entertaining. It is filled with wonderful things. It ensures that you never get bored when you are with nature.

Once you get close to nature, you will start experiencing its magical ways to help and support you.

Nature can be your best companion. When you feel alone, connect with nature to have the best company.

When you identify the development of mind, nature will bring you to the present and activate all your senses to eliminate the unmindfulness.

You will get creative ideas by learning the patterns of nature.

## Self-Affirmations

I am…………………………….. and I am deeply connected to nature. I choose to be near nature. I praise its beauty and tranquillity. I am committed to preserving the wonders of nature. I feel love toward all living creatures. My heart is filled with compassion and respect for every being in the natural world. I understand nature's rules and regulations. I embrace its decisions with patience. I am grateful for the gifts of nature.

*"The world is not to be put in order; the world is order, incarnate. It is for us to harmonize with this order."* - Henry Miller

# You with Resources

*"Do what you can, with what you have, where you are." - Theodore Roosevelt*

This seems to be simple, yet is a highly effective tool. We have so many things around us to use or misuse. Each item has a specific use and a right way to use it. "Use" and "the right way to use" are both important to be discussed. The things we can use for a specific purpose are called resources. There is no scarcity of resources in nature. They are scattered around us. Only it requires sharp eyes to identify these resources. It needs study and research to bring out the principles and inherent virtues of resources. At last, it needs skilled hands to proficiently utilize them. All these activities are core components of resourcefulness.

Resourcefulness is among the best capabilities a human can acquire. Often, it is considered superior to smartness by many intellectuals. It involves making choices or decisions based on your situation and the available resources. A resourceful person can think beyond his perspective. He can identify solutions that benefit both himself and others. Resourcefulness is about optimizing the options available to you. Creativity is different from resourcefulness because creativity involves not only creating something new but also improving existing things. Resourcefulness doesn't only mean a way to deal with scarcity. Instead, it is the virtue that leads to greater success. It is not something which should be reserved for hard times only. Instead, being able to do more with available resources and inspiring others to do the same is important. This approach of resourcefulness has enough potential to prevent challenges or hard times.

After going through the past, the history of resources teaches us that there is a specific time period for the importance of each resource. This shows that the use and value of a resource are generally not permanent. Therefore, the demand for a resource is often temporary. The demand for the most valuable resources of the past is not the same today. The resources we are using now may lose their importance in the future. Resourcefulness is the quality of understanding the real value of time, effort, and a particular resource.

The 21st century is an era of uncertainty. The world is a battleground and it is getting tougher every day to continue the fight. You need to be resourceful if you want to succeed in this era of competition. Resourcefulness should be a part of your daily life because it gives you choices in creating new ways to reach your desired destination.

When you acquire skills in planning, organizing, decision-making, problem-solving, and application of knowledge. These skills collectively form the core components of resourcefulness. When you can think of multiple outcomes of an activity, you can set clear objectives, you can experiment with new approaches, you have the ability to face upcoming challenges, and most importantly, you can establish connections between knowledge and its application to achieve desired goals, then only you are a resourceful person.

Resourcefulness demands more than intelligence. It requires the ability to process information emotionally as well as intellectually. Research indicates that a resourceful person not only achieves his goals but also responds strongly under stressful circumstances. Executive functioning skills play a significant role in learning how to regulate oneself and others. You can cultivate resourcefulness through the practice of being goal-directed. You can create an environment that improves resourcefulness within you and others. You can encourage yourself and others for planning, strategizing, prioritizing, goal setting, identifying resources, and monitoring progress in order to develop this trait.

Learning about resourcefulness from the biographies of famous and successful historical personalities can be one of the best ways. You will get to know that their common personality traits include seeing beyond fixed solutions and learning from mistakes along the journey. You need to create a balance between an individual's strength and a team's collective power in order to use resourcefulness in a system or team. You must know which tasks can be best accomplished by someone alone and which require teamwork. A resourceful person also knows the importance of positive scepticism. For being a resourceful person it needs the ability to explore many solutions to a single problem and it requires a healthy dose of doubt.

In the 21st century, you must command two specific resources: one for the real world and the other for the virtual world. Human resources are crucial in the real world. Knowledge of digital technology is essential in the virtual domain. Both are powerful and important resources. Let's learn about them one by one.

Let's begin with human resources for the real world. Human resource management is an approach to managing the workforce. Its main goal is gaining a competitive advantage through effective and capable employees. You need to determine the kind and size of the team for a specific task. You must possess the ability to attract and hire the best workforce. You must also ensure their engagement and productivity. You should work on empowering the workforce to acquire new skills for future challenges. Their efforts must be recognized and rewarded. Their achievements must be celebrated to keep the morale of the team high.

You must remember to maintain proper communication channels for all team members. The workplace should be kept clean, and there should be rules for health and safety. You should have a sense of responsibility for everyone working under you and their overall well-being. Always have a sense of morality that managing human resources is not about exploiting them; instead, it is about collaboration for the collective good.

Now, let's discuss the importance of digital knowledge and how to acquire it. This is the era of uncertainty, and it requires adapting quickly to the rapidly changing environment. It becomes essential to gain relevant knowledge and skills of digital technology. You must learn those things about technology that add value to your life. You can utilize easily available information in your desired way. You can also utilize the interconnectivity of various information sources. The best part of digital technology is that it allows you to learn anytime and anywhere. Digital sources can make the learning experience more efficient, engaging, and personalized. With these digital tools, you can learn anything, anytime, and anywhere. There are various types of digital tools available, full of creative and useful content. Also, there are many digital tools for communication and coordination that make it easier for you to connect with others. You can share your ideas and collaborate to reach solutions to problems.

I want to share my journey with the digital world for your better understanding. When I was introduced to the internet, it was hard for me to believe its power. I felt like it was an otherworldly experience with the internet. With time, by using the internet, many of its principles and capabilities were revealed to me. I used Google to enhance my English vocabulary and I succeeded. Google became my best friend. It still helps me check facts and find useful information. Even while writing this book, Google has been with me whenever I needed it. Google or the Google Guru, has been one of the best teachers in my life. Now we are introduced to a new digital technology, and that is Artificial Intelligence or (AI). Its purpose includes computer-enhanced learning, reasoning, and perception. Various industries are using AI today. Some critics fear and oppose the extensive use of advanced AI due to potential negative effects on the human species. The power of AI should not be underestimated. I strongly advise you to learn about AI. It will prove to be a strong tool in dealing with upcoming challenges. AI is the future, learn about it as much as possible.

## Self-Affirmations

I……………………………….. am a resourceful person. I can find the resources which I need to complete any task. I understand the real value of a resource. I know the right way to use resources efficiently. I am learning the importance of planning and organizing. I am efficient in using human, digital, and any other resources. I am always be ethical enough when using a resource.

*"Resourcefulness is the ultimate resource." - Tony Robbins*

# Power of Ignorance

*"The greatest enemy of knowledge is not ignorance, it is the illusion of knowledge." - Stephen Hawking*

Knowledge is the most crucial tool for human beings. Without knowledge, life can get out of control. Without knowledge, you cannot make decisions; instead, decisions will be made for you. History is full of examples to tell us that it is the lamb that is sacrificed, not the lions. With the power of knowledge, you can become the lion of the 21st century, and without it, be prepared to be sacrificed. In simple words, knowledge is the most powerful tool. We can only use something when we know about it. The more we know about something, the better we can utilize it. This art of using knowledge creates real power. However, dealing with knowledge is not as simple as we think. Like every coin has two sides, knowledge also has its pros and cons. There are both good and bad aspects to knowledge. Here, I will discuss some gray areas of knowledge.

Gathering too much knowledge is a problem of the present era. There's so much information out there, and it is impossible to know everything. Our curious minds keep looking for new things. We collect stuff we do not need. People are busy gathering tons of knowledge but they do not have time to use or work on it. So much information can create an extra burden on our brains and in that situation, it creates confusion and makes it hard to decide things. So, getting more and more knowledge doesn't always give us the best results. Social media makes this even more complicated. It is filled with lots of information that is tempting or attractive to our curious minds. Anyone can get and share information on it, so there's always something new. All that makes social media a huge source of information. If you are addicted to this information, then it will be tough for you to resist scrolling through social media.

The second issue with knowledge is its quality. We achieve the results according to the quality of the knowledge we have. Using the best knowledge brings the best outcomes. If we depend on outdated or low-quality information, it will lead us nowhere. Sometimes, this rotten knowledge can be even harmful to us. Rotten knowledge is like rotten food; it's better not to have it. We prefer to buy shoes from a branded company to ensure good quality, but unfortunately, we often compromise when it comes to the quality of knowledge. Social media bombards us with unwanted information. Many people think that it's free and useful for updating oneself on social media. They do not realize the game behind it. When something is free, then you are the product. Nothing comes without paying the price.

The third issue with knowledge is government interference in deciding what we should learn. As governments change, they change the curriculum or syllabus according to what suits to their ideology and policies. State-provided education creates ideal citizens and a workforce for its institutions and to run the national economy. They showcase educational achievements to attract votes. We can see their hidden motives in the government's educational policies and the functioning of government educational institutions. Here, I am not suggesting that public schooling is unnecessary, but my point is that it's not enough. It's not sufficient to fulfil your aspirations and your parents' dreams. You need to find your path to gather more useful knowledge from trustworthy sources. I hope that in the future, the situation will change and students will have more choices in what they can learn.

The solutions to the above-mentioned problems with knowledge lie in 'controlled ignorance'. It is not an obligation to know everything. You can use ignorance as a tool to bypass unwanted information. Before relying on any information, you must doubt the sources. You should always verify information and data. Don't blindly trust any source as it can mislead you. Here, my sincere advice to you is to be ignorant toward misinformation. Always avoid believing in false propaganda. Always stay aware and refrain from affirming unworthy beliefs in your subconscious mind.

When it comes to knowledge, it is essential not to rely completely on anyone and any source. It also includes the knowledge from your teachers and parents. Learn the art of using resources for knowledge according to your needs. You can diversify your knowledge sources to compare and adopt the best.

You should be a good magnet for attracting good quality of knowledge.

You can apply knowledge through experiments to see real results. The true quality of knowledge and information can only be obtained through experimentation and cross-checking. Keep what is valuable and useful and leave what is not. Original and useful knowledge becomes our strength, while false, misleading and filtered information can lead us to harm. 'What not to know' is also a part of knowledge. Ignorance can be dangerous but when we know how to use it, it becomes a powerful tool. In the 21st century, we cannot fight with outdated weapons. Similarly, we must be equipped with the best and latest knowledge. Curiosity is good, but the condition is that it should lead us to the best quality of knowledge. Controlled ignorance should be used to bypass unwanted information.

Here, I am giving you a wonderful example from our daily life. To remember the power of ignorance, think about how people read newspapers daily. A newspaper almost has 15-20 pages and it takes only 10-20 minutes to glance through it. If you have to read it word by word, it would take a minimum of 2-3 hours. We are smart when it comes to newspaper reading because we only read what is interesting or important to us. We often leave a significant part of the newspaper without even reading its headlines. We know which sections are important for us, such as editorials, sports and international news. This means we have mastered the art of skipping and ignoring unwanted news from the newspaper. We already know which parts should be overlooked. We can apply this skill in our day-to-day life. Always remember that controlled ignorance is a powerful tool. You need it in this era of information.

## Self-Affirmations

I am...........................and I affirm that I am able to differentiate between useful and useless knowledge. I always focus on quality over quantity. I protect myself against the influence of propaganda, misinformation, and misleading content. I choose critical thinking over blind acceptance. I trust my instincts to guide me away from deceptive influences. I am capable enough to question, verify, and cross-check information. My awareness protects me from any type of manipulation. I use the practice of controlled ignorance. I recognize its strength as a tool to bypass unnecessary and harmful knowledge from my life.

*"Not knowing is true knowledge." - Lao Tzu*

# Foundation of Friendship

*"A real friend is one who walks in when others walk out."*
*- Walter Winchell*

Being a social animal, Homo sapiens need support from others. People are correlated with each other to sustain their existence. They form relationships for mutual support. Friends are not blood-related but have strong and deep bonds among themselves. Friends accept us as we are but always wish and support us to become what we deserve to be. Our friends impact our lives in ways we cannot even imagine. We all need friends in both happy and hard times.

On happy occasions, we need friends to celebrate and enjoy. And in sad situations, we need friends to stand with us and support us. We need friends from the very start of life. We need friends to play with in our childhood, to study and learn together in school, to shape our dreams, and desires when we are in college, to motivate and inspire us to achieve what we desire in adulthood and to have a laughter sitting together after retirement. They stand together during our hard and struggling periods. We enjoy our success and happy moments with them.

If anything bad happens, friends are the first to stand in our support. Friends experience ups and downs together during the journey of life. Here, I hope you can see the importance of friends throughout our lives. Research has shown that the better the quality of one's friendships, the higher the possibility of that person's happiness. It is good to be and have a best friend for maintaining social well-being.

Everyone has friends, but it is not necessary that they have true ones. Many people come in disguise as friends, but they are not genuine. Among them some are opportunists, some are frenemies, and some are forged friends. While it is important to have friends, it is also a sensitive matter because there are both positive and negative possibilities with a friend. Thus, it becomes important to identify a true friend from the crowd of fake ones. Here, I suggest some ways to differentiate between a true friend and a fake friend. These are...

A person who does not show respect, love, and care for his parents may have difficulty being a genuine friend. And if someone prioritizes his parents, it indicates his potential as a good friend.

Low self-respect and self-esteem in an individual decrease the ability to be a true friend. On the other hand, someone who loves himself is likely to extend that love to others. Stability in a person is very important because that keeps friendships lasting for a long time.

A person with an addiction can influence others to adopt the same behaviour. It's similar to how a contagious disease can spread. I advise you to avoid such individuals. A friend without any addiction can act as a positive influencer, he keeps you away from engaging in any addictive behaviour.

If someone lacks clarity in what he is doing, he may intentionally or unintentionally point you in the wrong direction. An individual with clear goals is less likely to misguide others.

Dealing with a person with a strong ego can be challenging for you. A person with an ego often sees himself as the main character and may disregard the self-respect of others. I advise you to keep a distance from such individuals.

Avoiding a person with a selfish nature is the right decision. Selfishness always harms the strength of a friendship. Selfishness can lead to broken expectations. It creates toxicity in the relationship.

In friendship, loyalty is a crucial factor. A wise person always avoids unfaithful friends, and you should also do the same. It is very crucial to distinguish between genuine and artificial loyalty.

Don't make a person your friend who is lazy and spends his life being inactive. Nobody appreciates someone who doesn't work. Always prefer someone active and hardworking.

Don't give a crook or cheater a second chance. It is foolish to trust someone who intentionally breaks your trust without a valid reason. Once you identify the bad intentions of a person, it's best to keep your distance from them as soon as possible.

Criminals, habitual offenders, and troublemakers should always be avoided as friends. They can bring chaos into your life at any time.

Stay away from a habitual pessimist because their negative outlook can diminish your hope and create a gloomy atmosphere. While occasional moments of losing hope are normal, keep yourself away from a habitual pessimist.

Don't make a person your friend who is a manipulator. These types of people consistently try to influence your decisions. They always believe that they are right and that their decisions or suggestions are superior.

A narcissistic person loves himself more than anyone else and doesn't have concern for others. He may sacrifice someone for his small interests because he lacks empathy for others. Being around a narcissist is a bitter experience. Keep a narcissist away from you by maintaining your confidence and never make such a life spoiler your friend.

Be cautious about someone who is the friend of your enemy. An enemy's friend is an enemy. It's important to prioritize unfiltered friendships.

Avoid forming friendships with individuals who show more interest in your financial assets than you. True friendships should not be built on material gains.

Keep away people who are quick to judge others. A healthy friendship should be based on maturity and acceptance.

Do not make a person who puts conditions on your friendship. It's better to maintain friendships with those who value you for who you are.

Your behaviour significantly influences your relationship with anyone, especially with friends. It's crucial to handle this bond of friendship with care because it is built on trust, cooperation, mutual understanding, and respect for each other's interests. Friendship is not a one-sided relationship. Both parties should play their roles honestly. If you are fortunate to have a true friend, it becomes your responsibility to care for and nurture the friendship. Here are some suggestions on how you should behave with your friends.

You must speak kindly to your friend. Use words filled with affection, care, and respect. Avoid flattery; instead, be sincere in your expressions.

Always be prepared to help your friend. It's your duty to rescue your friend when they are in danger. A true friend stands by in times of need. Never abandon your brother or friend when they are facing tough times.

Share and create good moments with your friends. These memories will form a foundation for a strong friendship.

Assist and motivate your friend in achieving his goals. When he loses hope, it is your duty to encourage him and stop him from giving up.

If there is any misunderstanding, you must have a conversation to resolve it as soon as possible. Remember to listen carefully and speak openly. Don't hide anything. Communication is key to maintaining and restoring a healthy friendship.

You must not judge your friend because a judgmental attitude can create resentment. Friendship is naturally sweet, you need not make it bitter.

It is acceptable to have differences with friends. It is okay if your friend does not agree with you. Differences are common, and always consider them as common.

It is your responsibility to protect your friends from harmful habits and addiction. A true friend is someone who observes and notices even slight changes in his friend's behaviour.

When your friend does something commendable, praise them in front of others. But if he makes a mistake, tell him privately.

Be aware of your friend's emotional state. You must ensure that he is not going through anxiety and depression in solitude.

## Self-Affirmations

I am ………………………………. and I am aware of the impact friends have on my life. I choose friends who uplift and inspire me. I surround myself with good company which enhances my well-being. I am a loyal and supportive friend. I distance myself from people with addictions or bad habits. I keep away from frenemies, manipulators and opportunists. I am aware of the behaviour of narcissistic people. I value genuine friendship over superficial relationships.

*"A friend is someone with whom you dare to be yourself." - Frank Crane*

# High Five Way

*"Against the assault of laughter, nothing can stand."*
*- Mark Twain*

Everything we do is not for our survival. We do so many things to achieve happiness. Everyone wants to be happy. We feel happy when we get what we desire. We do hard work to earn not money but happiness. We dream and desire to be happy. We think and act for happiness. But after all the efforts, happiness seems to be temporary. Happiness comes with a smiling face and goes away dancing. We can be able to have possession of anything but when it comes to happiness, we suspect ourselves. We suspect ourselves because of the past experiences we had. Our past experiences tell us that happiness comes and goes and we cannot hold it permanently.

It's impossible to hold happiness permanently and that makes us a little nervous. We also feel confused when we think about which way to use to reach happiness and how to hold it for a long time. As we all are unique, we all have our own unique and different ways to get happy. The meaning, definition, and intensity of happiness also change from person to person. After reading this, you get to know that happiness is very complicated concept. That is not true, happiness is not complicated but we made it so. Happiness, by its true nature is simple. It is within reach for everyone. With very normal circumstances, anyone can reach happiness. It doesn't need you to have so much possession, knowledge, wealth, power, influence, health and wealth. God made happiness available for everyone, anywhere, anytime.

There are so many ways to be happy. Here I show you one of the best ways to be happy. I call this the "High Five Way". Like everyone, I also cannot be happy all the time. When I need happiness, I use this way and happiness visits me instantly. The high five is a body gesture when two people at the same time raise one hand each and push or slap the palm against the palm of the other person. The gesture is often preceded verbally by a phrase like Give me five or High five. It is a happy gesture and is used for showing gratitude and greeting. People also use it when they are happy and laughing.

Here I use a "high five" as a symbol of this very important concept or way of life. This is a very simple concept or way to lead a happy life. You can invite happiness anytime by applying this very simple concept and I guarantee happiness will visit you. This concept has two assignments to do ...

To help five beings(person, animal, plant etc.)

To have laughter with five people.

Our first task is to maintain our social and spiritual well-being. When we help someone, it brings so many favourable things for us. Remember one thing: when you help others, you help yourself. It fills you with a sense of satisfaction. You create a good group or friends circle by helping others, and that helps you deal with loneliness, anxiety, and stress. Helping others is a way to show gratitude for our creature. It involves so many psychological benefits. This increases your social values. You feel that your importance is rising around you. As it has immense benefits we must follow this way.

Our second task involved laughing. Laughing is considered as one of the best exercises by health experts. Laughing has immense physical, psychological, and emotional benefits. It keeps your bodies healthy. It keeps your body relaxed and your immune system strong. It keeps your heart strong and leads you to live a long and happy life. It also burns calories to maintain your body weight. It keeps your relations healthy and it brings you happiness as it triggers happy hormone endorphins. Laughter or humour is the best panacea for depression and anxiety.

This is how high five way of lifeworks. If you put to discipline it will bring you sweet fruits. So, make it a habit to use high five way of living life.

## Self-Affirmations

I am……………………………..and every day I make a positive impact on my social life by helping others. Laughter is my daily medicine. I share happiness and joy with those around me. I attract happiness by helping others. I am a source of support and comfort to those in need. I am surrounded by a circle of love and positive energy. I contribute to a happy and harmonious world through my positive actions. I help and have laughter with others at least five times in a day.

*"Help others achieve their dreams, and you will achieve yours." - Les Brown*

# Shadow of sexual behaviour

*"Guiding teenagers through their journey of sexual discovery requires not just answers but open conversations, trust, and a foundation of understanding that respects their autonomy and choices." - Unknown*

There is a documentary series on the Discovery Network's History Channel titled 'How Sex Changed the World'. In the series, there is archive footage and expert interviews. The series explores how sex has influenced the history of the world. "How Sex Changed the World" is based on the principle that sex is a powerful force of nature. The series reveals true stories of powerful individuals who made extreme decisions influenced by their sexual behaviour. These decisions affected a wide range of areas and people. These surprising stories illustrate how the sexual behaviour of powerful figures has shaped human history. I mentioned this example intending to raise awareness of the significant influence of sexual behaviour in our life.

We must recognize the importance of sex as it is the way to sustain life on Earth. We are all here due to the functioning of this natural phenomenon. It ensures the existence of every living species, including us, the Homo sapiens. Naturally, sex is a pleasurable experience, but it has enough power to both create and ruin life. When handled well, it has the power to create life. If could not manage it, it has the potential to ruin lives. That is why it becomes crucial to learn about sex and sexual behaviour.

The age of adolescence is called the age of storms. During this period, physical, mental, and emotional changes occur simultaneously. These changes create powerful storms in one's life. Adolescents are not always fully aware and able to handle these changes. They feel like there has been a complete change in their lives. At the beginning of this age, they lack the knowledge and emotional intelligence to handle these changes. Along with that they also feel pressure to think about their future and a successful career.

Almost every change poses challenges; it is the sexual changes that disturb the most. Adolescence opens up a new world. These changes occur in physical, mental, and emotional forms. The rush of sexual hormones into the body triggers these physical, mental, and emotional transformations of brain and body. Rather than teaching you biology, my aim is to raise awareness of these changes. Awareness about the sexual behaviour is must to face the challenges related to it.

Now I would like to introduce you to some sexual changes and challenge. I also suggest some suitable ways to respond to them. Here they are...

The most important thing to know about sexual changes is that they are natural and happen to everyone. Accept and welcome these changes as an integral part of your life. The more you embrace reality the easier it becomes to handle these changes. Stay aware of what is happening with you. Always observe and notice slight changes in your body and emotions without creating any resentment.

Our bodies are amazing gifts given to us by God. Show gratitude to God by loving and embracing the changes that naturally happen to you. Life is all about changes because there is nothing permanent. So, it becomes important to not think excessively about these sexual changes. Instead, divert your attention to the many other aspects of life that also need your consideration at the same time.

Another important tool to deal with these sexual changes is the 'power of ignorance'. These changes affect us negatively when we start exploring new and pleasurable experiences. The more you explore, the more you get trapped in this cycle. Instead of focusing on sexuality, you must explore life on a larger canvas. Life is vast and filled with diverse experiences. If you get stuck in the narrow focus of sexuality, you will miss out on a significant part of this colourful life.

In this digital era, offering sexuality has become a significant aspect of marketing strategy. The advertising industry is well aware of the influential nature of sexual desires. They use sexuality to manipulate individuals and promote product sales.

For them, women are nothing but only symbols of sexuality. Half-naked bodies of women are introduced as a way to capture the attention of the common man. This objectification of women is one of the main reasons for the crimes against them. I advise you to stay vigilant and aware of the manipulative tactics used by the advertising industry.

Most people in the 21st century use social media. Users want more followers and likes. Some of them post content with a lot of sexuality to grab attention. They create a desire for something new in people's minds. If you think you are smart, you should use social media less or avoid it altogether.

It is unfortunate but true that the porn industry is now a billion-dollar market. In 2022, the total revenue of this industry reached 1.1 billion dollars. People all over the world are suffering from addiction to porn videos. And the situation in Asian and African countries is more concerning. Porn addiction has become a significant challenge in the 21st century. It is nothing but the game of dopamine. The release of dopamine provides instant pleasure. When it is done frequently, it turns into an addiction. Newcomers might not realize the vastness of porn content on the internet. Their habit of exploring sexuality through porn videos can lead to severe psychological and physical health hazards. For a person addicted to porn it might seem like there is no way out. Porn addiction can negatively impact relationships, careers, self-confidence, self-esteem, willpower, energy and overall happiness. The only safe way to avoid porn addiction is to "not explore it" and be strict with that discipline.

Many adolescents receive their sexual knowledge from unhealthy conversations with friends, social media platforms, and various internet sources. These are not authentic sources. They can sometimes be misleading. It is important not to fully trust these sources. You should seek accurate information from trustworthy sources like parents, teachers, and properly licensed internet sources.

Instead of exploring sexuality, focus on exploring the importance of being active both physically and mentally. Always remember this insightful saying "an idle mind is the devil's workshop". Negative thoughts can quickly develop in the mind when we have nothing to do. Activeness is the most effective way to fight any form of addiction. Stay active and keep yourself occupied with work to prevent any type of addiction.

Know yourself — who you are? You are not what you think, feel or sense. Everything is temporary except your inner peace. You are your inner peace, you are consciousness. Don't chase pleasure instead stay with your peace. Pleasure needs a reason to make you feel good and has its negative after-effects. But inner peace is effortless and eternal.

Stay active by developing hobbies and interests. Invest your energy in learning new skills for positive purposes. You should engage in constructive activities. You should enrich your life by focusing on your personal growth. You can pursue creativity, sports, or acquiring knowledge but stay active. Only it contributes to a balanced and fulfilling lifestyle. It brings satisfaction and a sense of accomplishment.

Avoid living alone. Be part of a group, family or friends. Loneliness always welcomes an addiction. Being connected with others provides emotional support and a sense of engagement. It reduces the chances of falling into unhealthy habits. Social connections play a crucial role in mental well-being. It offers companionship and prevents the negative impacts of loneliness on one's overall health.

Be a gentleman and have dignified behaviour. Ensure that your behaviour should align with maintaining your character and self-respect. You should maintain decency in your actions and interactions to have healthy relations and self-image. You must be aware of how your behaviour reflects on your character. Your behaviour gets you respect from others.

Do not be friends with people dealing with sexual addiction. Stay away from those who struggle with this issue. It will be more beneficial to be around good people. Choose friends who create a positive impact on your life.

Before maturity, falling in love might not be good decision. Instead, focus on your career. After achieving career goals, you can think about being in a relationship. Going step by step can lead to a successful life.

## Self-Affirmations

I am................................ and I accept and embrace my body and behavioural changes. I avoid unnecessary sexual exploration. I engage in productive activities that uplift me. I only trust sexual knowledge from authentic and trustworthy sources. I prioritize my career before considering relationships. I consciously ignore unworthy sexual content on social media platforms. I live an active and busy life. I focus on only positive pursuits.

*"Guiding teenagers through the complexities of sexuality means creating an environment where questions are met with understanding, curiosity is met with education, and choices are met with support." – Unknown*

**ACCEPT**     **STOP**     **CREATE**

# Accept, Stop and Create Change

*"The first step toward change is awareness. The second step is acceptance." - Nathaniel Branden*

There are three dimensions in the universe we all know, but scientists consider time as the fourth dimension. Time has no relevance if there is no change. We can feel time just because we can feel changes around us. We discovered time by observing changes. That is how change is a very broad concept to understand. Here, we consider its relevance in our lives without going deep into science.

Humans have a general tendency to get attached to what is close to their hearts or belongs to them. There is also a tendency in humans to distance themselves from things they dislike. People resist changes in what they like and desire changes in what they don't. Sometimes they want to change and sometimes they don't.

Thus, they create a life full of confusion and contradictory thoughts, feelings, and emotions. The main reason behind this scenario is that people often don't know how to accept, stop, and create changes. These three words associated with change are magical. We can describe them as threegray-to-gold ways to deal with change. Here, we will discuss each of them separately.

**First, accept change.**

Many things happen in our lives over which we have no control. If we are too attached to someone or something we struggle to see any negative changes in their state. We experience pain when these negative changes occur. This pain continues until we accept the change. Acceptance and time are crucial for healing unwanted wounds and adapting to changes. Here, I suggest some ways to use this powerful tool.

- Acknowledge or accept reality, change, and circumstances as they are.

- Accept incoming thoughts, feelings, and emotions without any resentment. Let them come and go.

- Express your thoughts, feelings, and emotions if you want to. Expression lightens up the brain and body. Depression has only one solution, which is expression.

- Be in the present most of the time. Do what you can. Engage in activities to be in the present.

- Try to look at the positive side of the change. You will find something good if you can change your attitude.

## Second, stop the happening of any change

Many things around us change and many times we dislike those changes. Instead of passively watching undesired changes happening, we can actively intervene to stop them. Examples of changes that can be stopped include gaining weight, losing health, decreasing resources, breaking relationships, and wasting time. Mostly these changes are caused by habits and addictions. Here are some effective ways to stop changes.

- These types of changes occur as problems due to our ignorance. Analyze the situation thoroughly, make a plan, be prepared, and then follow your plan to come out of the situation. That is how you can stop that change from happening.

- Engage in daily physical exercises, yoga, and meditation to stop negative changes in your body and brain.

- To prevent negative changes in your financial stability, avoid extravagance and ensure income stability.

- Work on your communication skills and be humble to maintain relationships.

- Stay active, find meaningful activities, and avoid sitting idle. Use your time for something worthwhile.

- Distance yourself from bad habits and addictions. If you are engaged in them, leave them as soon as possible.

- Believe that you can stop changes that you don't like.

## Third, create change

We all have our dreams and desires in our lives, and all that can be possible by creating some positive changes. Without changes, we cannot get what we desire. This is the best approach for achieving dreams and desires. Here we must focus on only positive changes related to our dreams and desires. The only way to see the changes happening is by actively creating them. We can generate positive changes within our limits, and our limits are stretchable. Let's explore how to create positive changes in your lives.

- Be clear about your dreams and desires. Don't be confused. First, decide what to do, then only move on. It requires a positive attitude and thinking toward goals to achieve them. Think that it is happening.

- Have a proper plan to follow. First, plan the work, then work the plan.

- Hard work has only one substitute and that is smart work. Work smartly and use time and other resources wisely.

- Be fully focused on your work when you are going to create positive changes. You can use the flow state. That will make it effortless and quicker.

- You can develop a good set of habits to support your efforts to achieve your goals.

- You can learn new skills and build a support system for your confidence.

- Work on being physically, mentally and emotionally fit to put forth your best efforts.

## Self-Affirmations

I am ……………………………….. and I understand that change is a natural part of my journey. I accept the things I cannot change. I release resistance and trust in the acceptance of creating positive changes. I have the power to stop negative changes. I can prevent undesired outcomes which are in my limits. I am the architect of my destiny. I have the strength and willpower to create positive changes in my life. I attract opportunities for growth and success. I shape my reality by accepting, stopping, and creating changes.

> *"When we are no longer able to change a situation, we are challenged to change ourselves." - Viktor Frankl*

# Life is Colourful

*"Life is like a rainbow. You need both the sun and the rain to make its colors appear." - Unknown*

Life is not about black and white. It's colourful. A variety of colours is the real ornament of life. These colours make it incredibly beautiful. Our creator believes in variety, which is why the universe, nature, and our planet Earth are filled with varieties. Nothing created by our creator is superfluous; instead, everything has a particular role to sustain the continuation of the universe.

Look at the midnight sky, and you will see an ocean of stars. We still do not know the full extent of the universe and the secrets it holds. Nature is full of various living creatures in different geographical features. Our ecosystem needs this variety to sustain its existence. There are numerous animals, trees, water creatures, and microorganisms, and they all support each other to maintain life on this planet. This demonstrates that variety is a pattern in nature just as it is in the universe.

Our ancestors learned about this pattern by observing nature. They incorporated variety into their culture. They adopted a nomadic lifestyle and discovered multiple sources of food. They also adapted to extreme weather conditions and seasons. They developed various tools and instruments to perform different tasks.

But unfortunately, in the last few centuries, we have broken the rule set by nature. The rule suggests incorporating variety into things and life. The rule which is designed to sustain our existence. Instead, we have embraced specificity—the specificity of everything. We have been trained in this way by influential powers. Every aspect of life has been contaminated by the viral disease of being specific. Competition has played a significant role in establishing specificity in society. Now we are specific in what we learn, what we do, what we have, how we behave, in career selection, in relationships, and everywhere else.

Consider this through the example of a machine. A specific part of a machine serves a specific purpose. Once this part malfunctions or becomes outdated, it will be discarded. Now, we are also functioning like parts of a machine. Once we lose our relevance, we may be discarded. We will be treated similar to the part of a machine. This can put us and our dependents into the struggle for existence.

The 21st century and the era that follows will be dominated by machines equipped with artificial intelligence. These machines are capable of performing a wide range of tasks. Only a few will benefit from these machines. The rest may suffer if proper safety measures are not implemented. Governments must make some crucial decisions, and individuals should also be aware and able to face these challenges.

This is also an era of uncertainty. Where anything could happen anytime, anywhere. The population is reaching its peak and makes us more vulnerable. The sad part is that all the resources are controlled by a few. It feels that we are being trapped, and our tendency toward specificity can make the circumstances more severe. There are numerous other aspects of life where our monotonous and specific attitudes lead to sadness and make life boring.

Here I would like to give you a few pieces of advice to stay safe from the specificity of the 21st century.

Accept and adopt the varieties. There are varieties in culture, caste, religion, behaviour, mood, food, occupation, social status, hobbies, interests, entertainment, education, skills, and many more. Accept them as they are. Don't be particular until your safety, security, and significant interests are not compromised.

Learn more skills. This is the era of uncertainty. If you acquire diverse skills, it will be far easier for you to survive. Don't depend on others. Whatever is essential for survival, learn to be self-sufficient.

Explore multiple career options. In this era, relying on a single source of income is not sufficient. You must try to develop multiple sources to earn a livelihood.

Have multiple locations to live, and there should be a significant distance between them. Global geopolitics is not reliable as it keeps changing. Any decisions of global power can create severe effects on the people of any specific locality. You should try to develop more options to be safe from a natural or man-made calamity. These calamities are so powerful that they can hit us hard. Have a passport and visit many countries because it will be safer if you have multiple locations to live worldwide.

Explore different things in life. Life has many enjoyable experiences, so try various activities. Don't stick to just one, enjoy the variety. Make your life more colourful by trying different things.

Choose a different occupation than your family members. Add variety if possible. Do not simply copy any of your family members. Instead, explore new opportunities. You must create your life journey with more variety and enriched experiences.

Create a group of your friends for multiple resources. Help others to receive help in return. Don't be egoistic and selfish. If you are, then you will live alone and suffer alone. No one will be there to help you when you face hard times.

You need to know about various aspects of life. You must also keep updating yourself. You never know when you will need what to sustain your existence. Use the powerful tool "ignorance" wisely. Don't gather what is of no use. Put variety in the knowledge that is essential for survival.

You have multiple aspects in your life. Don't stick to one and ignore others. Give equal importance to all aspects of your life.

Be aware of your investments. Diversity in your investment is mandatory in the 21st century. Any of your investments can fail at any time. Develop multiple options for investment.

**Self-Affirmations**

I am………………………………….. and I celebrate the colourfulness and diversity of life. I enjoy every aspect of my life with variety. I am dedicated to learning multiple skills. I create diverse income sources for more stability. I face life's uncertainties by creating multiple options for it. I appreciate the richness that variety brings to my life. I paint my life with colours of diverse experiences. I embrace a colourful life which is full of varieties.

> *"Life is a colouring book, and you hold the crayons."*
> *- Unknown*

# You, Your Choices and Your Destiny

*"Life is a matter of choices, and every choice you make makes you." - John C. Maxwell*

Our lives are shaped by the choices we make. Everything we have and experience is a result of decisions we have taken before. Every day, we face circumstances where we have to make choices. Whether we like or not, we have to make choices. These choices move our lives forward, like the wheels of a vehicle. Each decision of our past, present, and future forms life. Think of choices as the building blocks of our life story. Every choice shapes our destiny and determines the course of our journey. We must understand and recognize the importance of our choices. The right choices give us the power to face challenges in life more efficiently.

Our choices have a big impact on how we think and feel. They are a really important part of our lives. They affect our brain, body, emotions, and even our senses. When we make decisions, we are either taking control of our path or letting others decide for us. We cannot ignore the fact that choices are directive tools of our lives. We make choices not only to survive but also to actively participate in our own life story. Even if we do not choose or decide on something, it is also a choice. You should understand that choices help you to be in charge of your life.

Choices are always in variety. Choices can be strong or weak, nice or bad. The best choices will bring the best results. If you make the wrong choices, you might not get what you want. You will definitely get what is destined with the choices you made. It becomes important to pick wisely the right choice for achieving success. You must master the art of choosing. To lead a successful life, it is essential to become skilled at making the right choices. Your right choices shape the path to the life you want to live. Here are some "Gray to Gold" tips to make better choices:

1. Listen to what feels right in your instincts.

2. Do not let your mind to push you into making bad choices.

3. Strong decisions lead to good places. You must put effort into making your decisions strong.

4. You must pay full attention when you are going to make a choice. Don't make any choice with a careless attitude.

5. Take charge of your choices. Your choices are your responsibility. No one else can do anything with your choices without your consent.

6. Learn from your mistakes if you have made bad choices. Don't let the same mistake repeat.

7. Always prioritize good choices. You must have a strong belief that your right choices will bring good things to you someday.

8. Keep emotions and feelings in check. The impact of your choices will last longer than your emotions and feelings.

9. Think about other aspects like time, knowledge, skills, and resources before making any choice.

10. Ask questions (why, when, where, what, and how) to make choices clearer.

11. Build a habit of making the supporting grid of good choices. One right choice will support another right choice.

## Self-Affirmations

I am……………………….. and I trust my instincts while making any choice. I make choices that are suitable for my overall well-being. I am in full control of my decisions and choices. Each choice I make contributes to my growth and happiness. I avoid bad and unworthy choices that hinder my progress. I am free from the grip of addictive choices. My wisdom guides my decisions. I take responsibility for my choices. I am empowered by nature to make conscious, wise, and positive choices.

> *"You are free to choose, but you are not free from the consequence of your choice." - Ezra Taft Benson*

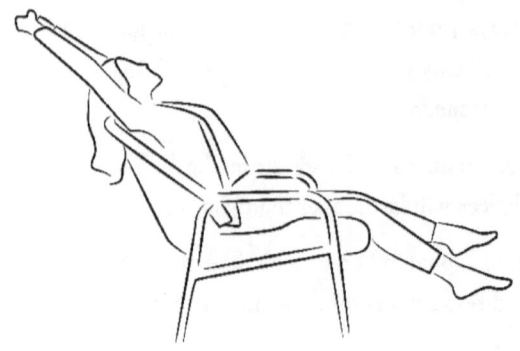

# Relax to Regain

*"Rest when you're weary. Refresh and renew yourself, your body, your mind, your spirit. Then get back to work." - Ralph Marston*

There is a day and night system given to us by nature. The day is designated for work and the night for rest. Like every living organism, we humans, also need rest. Rest is a natural requirement of the brain and body. It is crucial for maintaining our body's health, regaining strength, and repairing any broken functionalities of the body and brain. Rest is as important for good health as diet and exercise. It improves the performance of the brain and body. Rest also prepares the brain for learning, remembering, and creating. When we are resting our brain acts almost like a kidney. It removes negative toxic elements from our bodies.

Every part of the body has a system to repair damages and allow us to heal and regain health. These repair processes start working when we rest. If we don't get enough rest, then these natural repairing processes are disrupted. Insufficient quality rest gradually increases the risk of many diseases and disorders. This cause problems for the brain and heart. Therefore, it becomes crucial to consider the role of rest in our lives. However, this is not what I am trying to explain to you here in this chapter.

I hope we have adequately discussed the importance of rest before and after any action. Before proceeding further, I would like to ask some questions.

Can you relax while running?

Can you relax while playing?

Can you relax while studying?

Can you relax while speaking?

Can you relax while working?

Possibly, you might say "No," but that is not true. We have a gifted functional system to rest while doing any action. From now on, we will discuss relaxing while doing any work. This is a wonderful and magical skill to learn. You will get significant outcomes from this practice. It works when we use certain techniques while working. Here are the "Gray to Gold "tricks to follow.

Relieving tension in the brain and body.

Increasing mental and physical flexibility.

Slowing down the speed of doing work.

Practicing controlled breathing, inhaling, and exhaling.

Exhaling negative thoughts, feelings, and emotions while inhaling positive thoughts, feelings, and emotions.

Creating a balance between work and the available energy flow.

This way of working is highly effective. It serves as an important tool to deal with various situations on a daily basis. Now, let me mention the immense benefits of relaxing while doing any work.

1. It increases productivity manifold.

2. It boosts confidence and strengthens willpower.

3. It keeps the brain and body fit.

4. It increases agility in any action.

5. It maintains a high metabolism rate and energy level.

6. We can work for a long time without getting tired.

7. It enhances mental and physical stamina.

8. It makes you a warrior who is invincible.

## Self-Affirmations

I am……………………………….and I prioritize proper relaxation as an essential elements of my well-being. I maintain my overall health and vitality by resting in between activities. I relieve mental and physical tension while working. I create a balance between energy and work to be done. I know the benefits of breathing in the right way while working. I can balance the speed of doing any work with the energy flow. I allow myself the time needed to relax, recharge, and rejuvenate. I create a foundation for health, strength, and inner peace through relaxation.

*"Rest is not merely a matter of doing nothing. It is rather allowing the soul to speak, to think, to dream, to live its inner life in the stillness of the night." - Thomas Merton*

# You with Others

*"We judge others by their behaviour. We judge ourselves by our intentions." - Ian Percy*

Homo sapiens are excellent in social engineering. We can cooperate, coordinate, and harness collective power for our common good. Our capabilities arise from our behaviour. Our behaviour is a gift from nature that provides us with various options for different circumstances. The achievements of humanity originated with the help of these behavioural options. Our behaviour is one of the key factors that enables us to thrive.

The science behind behaviour is very simple. Behaviour is the way someone acts. It's an action aimed at creating, changing, and maintaining something. It serves as a response mechanism to internal or external circumstances. Quality, intensity, and quantity are the basic key parameters of behaviour. A significant chunk of human behaviour is of unconscious or subconscious origin. Only a small part can be consciously controlled. There is no need to worry, you can train your unconscious or subconscious behavioural responses. You only need consistent practice and the establishment of good habits.

If you look at the past, it is filled with many examples of individuals who are experts in human behaviour. They all have specialized techniques for dealing with the most complicated species, that is Homo sapiens. Here, I would like to share with you some "Gray to Gold" behavioural techniques to transform your gray areas into golden opportunities. You can use these approaches to be the best at human behaviour.

Don't expect anything from anyone. Expectations are the worst things to develop in one's behaviour. They bring bitterness to relationships. They initiate negative outcomes and hinder mutual assistance. Expectations block cooperation and coordination. If your expectations from others are high, it indicates that you lack skills in behaviour. People tend to be with those who have low expectations from others. Best you can do is replace expectations with acceptance.

Do not be overly reactive. Your reactions are a crucial part of your behaviour. If needed, give proper and conscious reactions. Reactions have the power to build or destroy. Take time before reacting to something.

Ego is the biggest enemy of a person. When it crosses the limit of self-respect, it becomes problematic. It creates an unhealthy atmosphere for the person suffering from ego issues. Ego negatively impacts facial and body expressions. If you have control over your ego, you can attract more people into your life. People feel safe around those with no ego.

Speak less, listen more. Everyone wants to express themselves in front of others. If you give them a chance to speak or express, they feel good about you. The feeling of being heard is amazing. If you let them express themselves, it will bring you into their good books.

Never complain, condemn nor criticize anyone. Everyone is in love with himself, and his self-respect is precious to them. When you try to destroy or damage his self-image or ego, he can become furious or feel resentful toward you. If you want to influence someone, you must respect his self-image.

Never engage in an argument. Arguments are entirely futile, a waste of time and energy. It always leaves behind a negative impression. Arguing is the fool's way. If you are a wise person, always avoid it. An argument leads nowhere. Never be overly excited and ruin a fruitful discussion. Stay calm and composed while discussing anything with anyone.

Always praise, appreciate, and recognize the efforts made by someone. This is the best way to deal with any person. Everyone wants to be liked and praised. Everyone wants to be appreciated for their efforts and achievements. Everyone wants their work to make a difference. So always be broad-hearted when it comes to praising or recognising someone's efforts.

What you feel shows on your face. Your face is the mirror that reflects what is going on inside you. All emotions like love, anger, happiness, sadness, hatred, jealousy, ego, and eagerness have a way of expressing. Feeling good to express well is the formula. It doesn't mean that you should hide your feelings or emotions. You cannot hide strong emotions, and if you try, it will consume much of your energy and you will not be able to get the desired results. Always remember that for positive expression, you need to feel good. Again, remember to feel good.

Always be ready to help. Helping is the best way to create new relationships and maintain old ones. A helpful nature is the most accepted value in society worldwide. But always remember one thing: "Help without expectations".

Learn the art of making expressions more dramatic. Usually, speaking without fluctuations in voice and avoiding body language creates boredom. No one likes to be bored. To avoid boredom, make your expressions more dramatic. People are more interested in presentation skills than content.

Use sense of humour. Humour is like the fragrance emanating from your behaviour. Humour has the power to accomplish the hardest things most efficiently. It serves as a safety valve. You can manage anything with the help of humour. If you find anything hard to say, you can express it through humour. Humour keeps you in the present moment. Humour is the best habit to adopt and the best skill to become adept at.

To be interesting, show the same interest in others. It is a barter system when it comes to interest. Do not think of anything only from your perspective. You should also consider other people's point of view. Understanding creates similarities with someone. You will receive what you give to others. Show others that you care for them. The deal between you and someone should not be one-sided.

Learn body language. It is an art and a skill. Be a master of it. You can enhance your expressions by using the right body gestures. Being skilled in noticing slight changes in someone's facial or body expression can give you an extra advantage.

Create eagerness. If you want someone to behave appropriately, try to create eagerness in them to do things in your desired way. Let the person think that they do it because they want to. Everyone prefers to behave independently. Don't force anyone to do something. Don't try to overpower their will. Instead, you should create eagerness in them if you can.

You can also learn advanced behaviour skills through the study of human behaviour and psychology.

## Self-Affirmations

I am.............................. and I help others without expecting anything in return. I inculcate genuine kindness and generosity in myself. I am a master of body language. I use dramatic expressions in my interactions with others. My behaviour leaves a positive impact on those around me. I always praise and appreciate the efforts of others. I recognize others' contributions. I never complain, condemn nor criticize anyone. I accept others without having any intentions to change them.

*"In the intricate dance of human behaviour with others, empathy is the melody that harmonizes relationships, connecting hearts across the rhythm of understanding." – Unknown*

# Overview of Social Media

*"Social media is about sociology and psychology more than technology."* - Brian Solis

This era is the era of information. After the invention of the internet, it has become very easy to access any information with a single click. In a short period, the internet has created an unimaginable impact on how people live their day-to-day lives. It gives the human species the capability to explore new ideas, information, and endless possibilities. With various other things, the internet introduced social media to us. Social media is a medium for interactions where people can create, share, and exchange information. Social media has numerous pros and cons, opportunities, and adversities. In this chapter, we will begin by exploring the advantages of social media when it is used efficiently.

Anyone can publish their ideas and creativity.

It helps in making friends and finding old disconnected friends.

It is a source of free information that we can use for various aspects of life.

It is the best and fastest communication medium. It keeps us updated about what is happening in the world.

It helps in growing one's business, developing a career, and earning through social media.

It can provide us with updated knowledge and enhance our capabilities.

It helps in understanding the truth because we can access information about both sides of the coin.

Social media platforms are entertaining and allows us to discover our hobbies and interests.

It can save information and memories for us.

Although social media is very useful and necessary in the 21st century, at the same time, it also has some severe side effects. If you don't use social media wisely, it can cause harm to you. Almost 85 percent of the total world population is using smart phones. The majority of them have accounts on various social media platforms. They are the first users of social media. They are doing it without knowing how much to use it. They are unaware of the after-effects of social media on individuals and society. Here are the harms of social media platforms.

Social media user can become addicted to it. Almost 10 percent of total users are highly addicted to using social media.

It is just a way to "kill time" if used without any purpose. The popularity of this pastime has increased significantly over the last decade.

It can be misused for spreading misinformation, which has enough power for destruction.

Your data and information could be misused by others. There are so many who are using various ways to collect your data to misuse it. Your data are also used for profit in the advertisement industry.

It can also lead you to physical and psychological problems. It can cause you anxiety, depression, sleeplessness, low willpower, and inactivity.

Social media is also a platform for cyber bullying and cybercrime. It is full of active hackers.

These platforms are being used massively for spreading religious, ideological, and political propaganda. This can cause polarization in society.

After all the discussion, I hope you are now sufficiently aware of the use and misuse of social media. You are also aware of the addictive behaviour associated with social media use. You are not entirely safe on these platforms because there are many vultures ready to prey on you. It is crucial not to have too much trust in these platforms. Your personal information is precious, so keep it safe. Always avoid sharing your personal and private information on these platforms. Use social media for your benefit. If you can't do it, then abstain from it. If you do not use it in controlled way, you will be used by social media.

## Self-Affirmations

I am……………………….and I am aware of the time I spend on social media. I ensure social media adds value to my life. My personal information is precious and I guard it. I am aware of the addictive nature of social media. I am vigilant against misinformation. I critically evaluate the content I encounter on social media. I avoid comparison and negativity on social media. I refrain from sharing sensitive personal information online. I always ensure my safety in the digital world. I am in control of my social media use. I only use it as a helping tool.

> *"Social media is not just an activity; it is an investment of valuable time and resources." - Sean Gardner*

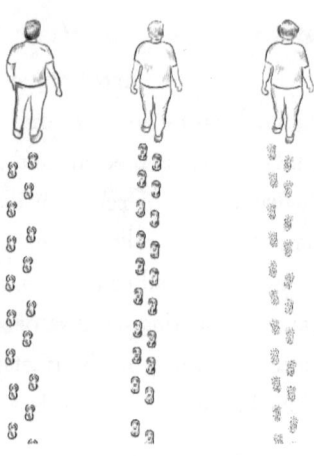

# Find out Patterns

*"Nature is an endless combination and repetition of a very few laws." - Ralph Waldo Emerson*

It is a misleading fact that we don't know what will happen next. We think we are unaware of the future and feel unable to face this so-called uncertainty. I believe that to some extent, we can predict the future. The universe is working on some patterns. From our ancestors to the current generation, we are learning these patterns. We are doing so because we want to predict the future. Certain patterns exist for specific purposes. These patterns are created by the universe to show us a path to predict the future to some extent. Only a few things happen beyond these patterns, we may be unaware of them. Some of these patterns are visible, while others may remain ambiguous. A pattern is nothing more than the repeated or regular way in which something happens or is done. Patterns are responsible for maintaining regularity in the world. We can see patterns in nature, human-made designs and abstract ideas. The core elements of a pattern involve repetition or following a fixed manner.

A geometric pattern is a repetition of geometric shapes. Patterns prevalent in nature are often chaotic and rarely exactly repeating. But we can observe the underlying pattern in any natural creation. A design pattern is a reusable architectural outline that is used for increasing the speed of any particular project.

Every work has a specific pattern to follow for a productive outcome. If you follow these patterns, you can get the desired benefits. For that, you need to uncover the hidden patterns first. You can try to get help from experts to learn the skills required for identifying the specific patterns of particular tasks. You can train yourself to deal with these patterns effectively. It needs hard work, practice, and patience. If you are ready to do it, you can become a master of these patterns. A person's intelligence is reflected in the number of patterns he knows. A person's power is determined by how effectively he applies these patterns.

If we talk about human behaviour, it is also not entirely unpredictable. There are certain hidden patterns in the behaviour, thinking process, and actions of a particular person. To some extent you can anticipate how a person will behave in a specific situation. You can speculate on possible thoughts in his head and predict his actions and reactions. Understanding these hidden patterns in human behaviour requires observation. First you have to collect information to uncover hidden pattern. You can create a profile to predict someone's behaviour, thinking and actions.

You can see different types of behavioural patterns. These behaviours include passive or active participation, friendliness or enmity, confident or hesitant nature, calm or short-tempered, self-love or self-sabotage, attraction or hatred. Some behaviours can be learned through experience. Most importantly, the factor to determine learned behaviour is a person's social background. He can be conditioned to act in a certain way. These learned behaviour patterns can begin to shape in childhood. For example, if someone has been raised in a household where someone suffers from anxiety or depression, their children, through learned behaviour may follow patterns which lead to anxiety and depression. This can be possible that their children may have depression or anxiety because it is their learned behaviour.

Learning, studying, and understanding patterns could prove to be among the best habits you can have. Always be observant and interested in learning, studying, and understanding the patterns hidden in nature, systems, tasks, processes, and the behaviour of yourself and others.

## Self-Affirmations

I am…………………………………and I am observant and interested in learning, studying and understanding the patterns. I observe specific patterns and then seek to understand them. I learn patterns from their basics. I first identify hidden patterns before engaging in any task or activity. I observe human behaviour and identify fixed patterns. I am also aware of my behavioural patterns. If my behavioural patterns needs to be repaired, I do it immediately. I use patterns for the common good of myself and others.

*"In the study of behaviour and systems, patterns are the fingerprints of predictability, guiding us through the labyrinth of human interaction and societal structures." – Unknown*

# You are Unique

*"You are not a drop in the ocean; you are the entire ocean in a drop." - Rumi*

Nature is full of diversity because it is essential for the survival of all species. Without that diversity, ecosystems become more vulnerable to severe change and challenges. Everything and everyone is playing their unique role in sustaining the functions of nature. If we talk about art, it thrives on uniqueness. The hunger of an artist to create something that has never been seen or experienced before is the real reason behind creativity and innovation. The beauty of any art is implicit in its uniqueness.

The same principle applies to the social life of humans. Everyone is different from another. They are different or unique in behaviours, appearances, talents, and contributions to society. What we think, what we do, and what we desire are not the same. Every individual develops their perspective by the way they experience and face the world.

Every good and bad experience depends on our actions. We create the strength and weakness for ourselves. No one is responsible for our triumphs and failures. People become what they choose and their uniqueness is created and ensured by all the choices they make. The important factor in shaping a person's identity, is their urge to feel unique, special, and different from others.

You are unique and uniqueness is your basic nature. You should not try to be or look like someone else. It's impossible to be the exact copy of anyone and there is no need to do so. Everyone has a different background, circumstances, and talents. There is no need to compare yourself with others. Comparison is the main cause of sorrow. It is the origin of ego and humiliation. Don't let comparison separate your uniqueness from your identity.

People tend to showcase the best parts of their lives on social media platforms. It is only a small part of their lives that is available on these platforms. Everyone has different abilities and talents. Sachin Tendulkar cannot be compared with Amitabh Bachchan. You cannot compare a monkey with a fish. Life is like a drama and everyone is playing their role. You cannot play all the roles. If you try to do so, you will fail. Instead, try to explore your abilities and talents by accepting your uniqueness.

Focus on yourself so that you can play your role in the best way. If you are not like others, that's okay. It is the thing that secures your uniqueness. This creates circumstances that are important for your talent to thrive. Uniqueness helps your talent grow. Then your talent will keep you unique. You can find out your talent by using these "Gray to Gold" methods.

Just reflect on your past and create your short life story. Emphasize the areas where you feel great, successful, and active. This process will help you discover your talent.

Self-evaluation and self-analysis are useful tools to uncover your hidden talents. Consider the work you enjoy the most. It's crucial that you love what you do.

Spend some time alone and open your mind to all possibilities. This makes it easier for you to choose what suits you best.

Learn new skills or upgrade old ones into real talents. Always remember that it requires time and effort to uncover your talent.

Engage in new activities to uncover your talent. They can open up new possibilities for you. Try things you have never done before.

Travel to explore yourself and your capabilities. The journey will enhance your knowledge and provide you with new experiences.

Seek input from others or consult experts. Sometimes, people know more about you than you know about yourself.

Accept new challenges. They create circumstances for your talent to thrive.

Always be ready to change yourself and your perspective. Sometimes, your attitude creates a distance between you and your talent. You have to reach out to your talent; your talent will not come to you.

## Self-Affirmations

I am ………………………………….. and I accept my uniqueness. I strongly believe that there is nothing like me. My talent makes me unique. I find my talent by exploring my past. I uncover my hidden talents through self-evaluation and self-analysis,. I accept new challenges that create circumstances for my talents to thrive. I am committed to secure my uniqueness. I am always ready to change my perspective if needed.

*"You were born an original. Don't die a copy." - John Mason*

# Hunting Pleasure or Self

*"Excessive pleasure is bound to end in pain."* - *Euripides*

We all want to be happy because happiness is our ultimate goal. We face many challenges to find that happiness. We feel joy when we get what we want, but this happiness doesn't last long. After a few days or months, we again get trapped in the web of negative feelings or sadness. Negative thoughts, emotions, and feelings can replace our happiness with sadness. This is a cycle of happiness and sadness. The mistake people make is not realizing the difference between happiness and pleasure. Happiness is something that lasts forever. It comes from within us and it does not depend on outside things. It always stays with us and does not need any specific conditions. On the other hand, pleasure is temporary and comes from external objects around us. Pleasure is a short-term addictive experience triggered by the secretion of brain's dopamine hormone. We should know and remember this difference for happiness that lasts longer.

Our dreams, desires, and achievements are the result of how we deal with good and bad experiences. Smart people are ready to go through some tough times to be happy in the long run. People who don't have clear goals or strong determination go after pleasure. We all naturally want good feelings and don't want bad ones, and this affects many choices we make. It is okay to want good things into your life, but it is not ok to go after pleasure too much. This habit can make other parts of your life worse. The excess of everything is bad and it is also true for pleasure. You must find the balance between pleasure and pain in order to live a balanced life.

There is nothing insightful in pleasure because important lessons don't come from enjoyable activities. The habit of hunting pleasure can lead you to engage in harmful behaviours. The most valuable lessons often come from tough times. Tough times are like our best teachers. Pain and work can coexist, but you cannot balance pleasure and work. When your life is dominated by pleasure, you will have less interest in working. Someone once said that pain is delayed pleasure and pleasure is delayed pain. It is always better to choose pain than pleasure. Pleasure makes it difficult to use your senses properly, and without senses, you cannot work efficiently.

Resting too long, eating unhealthy food, always being on social media, watching TV shows, aimless walks and talks, and other pleasurable activities can create chaos in your life. It's fine to enjoy fun stuff at some extent. If you go beyond limits, even the best things stop being enjoyable. It is important to be careful about how much time you spend on these activities. Feeling good is okay, but it should be within limits. We cross limits when we give up important things just to go back to enjoyable experiences. Too much pleasure can lead you to give up because you only seek a life of pleasure. You create a pattern of giving up as a way to get what feels good or pleasurable.

If you feel that you are in the habit of choosing pleasure over important tasks, it is time to be serious. You must be aware of how you react to enjoyable things. The solution is only to focus on your dreams. You should spend time on pursuing your goals. Get interested in your work to somehow stay busy. Accept the challenge of working toward your dreams over instant pleasure. Find happiness in activities that are part of your goals. Always remember that too much pleasure is an addiction. Try hard to break free from the habit of running after pleasure.

## Self-Affirmations

I am……………………….. and I always prioritize work over temporary pleasure. I am free from the grip of pleasure. I can control my choices and decisions. I believe that real happiness comes from purposeful actions. I can resist the allure of pleasures. I find satisfaction in facing challenges rather than getting quick pleasure. I am resilient against the temptation of pleasure. My happiness is derived from genuine achievements, not from momentary fun.

*"The secret of happiness, you see, is not found in seeking more but in developing the capacity to enjoy less." – Socrates*

# What feels Negative is not necessarily negative

*"Negative emotions like loneliness, envy, and guilt have an important role to play in a happy life; they're big, flashing signs that something needs to change." - Gretchen Rubin*

I strongly believe that whatever the supreme power has created holds significance. There is nothing purposeless. Everything we can feel, perceive, and imagine serves a logical importance in this efficient system of nature. Each particle has a specific role to play. Every particle is like a crucial part of a machine. We are in the habit of categorizing things as good or bad based on our experiences and interests. There is nothing purposeless in nature. If anything seems useless, it is your fault that you do not know its special nature. You should know how to utilize things in a particular way for the common good.

Sometimes you feel good and other times you feel sad. You like certain thoughts, feelings, and emotions. There are certain types of thoughts, feelings, and emotions that you do not like. There is no reason for this, but we unnecessarily classify our thoughts, feelings, and emotions as positive or negative, good or bad. Fear is often considered the root of all negative thoughts, feelings, and emotions. Suppose there is no fear within us, would it be possible to survive? The answer is negative. Fear is a natural element that keeps us safe from danger. Without being a little selfish, self-care becomes challenging. Ego gives us a sense of uniqueness. Ambitions serve as foresight for the future. Hatred keeps us safe from contamination and a little mercilessness is crucial for survival. Guilt prevents us from repeating mistakes, and sadness moderates our ambitions. Anger can settle disputes and create order. A sense of inferiority controls our extended ego. A sense of insecurity alerts us and keeps us safe from adverse events. These so-called negative thoughts, feelings, and emotions serve as indicators that something wrong is happening or may happen around us. They may feel painful but they work as a warning system. They let us know that there is an issue we need to address without wasting much time.

Negative emotions are not always detrimental. A person experiencing negativity toward such thoughts, feelings, and emotions may simply lack the skill to handle and manage them effectively. Everything mentioned above is a part of emotional intelligence. Emotional intelligence is a crucial requirement in this uncertain 21st century. The current generation lacks skills in dealing with emotional challenges. It requires emotional awareness, emotional expression, and emotional regulation to deal with emotional challenges. Now is the time to offer you some "Gray to Gold" ways to transform negativity into positivity and manage these emotions skilfully.

Be conscious and aware of your thoughts, feelings, and emotions.

Identify the origin of the so-called negative thoughts, feelings, and emotions.

Take them as an indication of something that needs to be addressed.

Avoid resentment toward negative thoughts, feelings, and emotions. Let them come and go without any struggle.

Don't let yourself be trapped in them. Observe them from a distance.

Work on the root cause of negativity. This is how you can start working on the issue.

Excess of anything is bad. Don't overly focus on negative thoughts, feelings, and emotions.

Identify unreasonable thoughts, feelings, and emotions, and then stop giving them excessive attention.

## Self-Affirmations

I am..................................................... and I am consciously aware of my thoughts, feelings, and emotions. I identify the origins of negative thoughts, feelings, and emotions to understand them better. I view them as indications of areas in my life that need my attention. I observe these negative thoughts, feelings, and emotions from a distance. I understand that excessive focus on negativity is unhealthy. I recognize unreasonable thoughts, feelings, and emotions. I can redirect my attention toward positivity.

*"It's okay not to be okay as long as you are not giving up."*
*- Karen Salmansohn*

# Smart Speaking

*"The most important thing in communication is hearing what isn't said." - Peter Drucker*

This universe has given all of us human beings a wonderful gift, the gift of expression or the gift of articulation. Humans can articulate or express their thoughts and feelings freely. This ability plays an important role in bringing us together. The power of speech helps us in deal with numerous circumstances. It is a famous saying that depression has only one solution that is expression. Expression proves to be a crucial in addressing anxiety and depression. Now you know its significance, you must handle this ability with care. When you use it efficiently, expression becomes a helpful tool. When you use it carelessly, it can turn into a self-harming weapon. In this chapter, we will learn about the art of speaking. We will also explore its various parts and aspects.

You may have encountered one-sided conversations. You may have also witnessed arguments of various intensities. People often seem more inclined to speak than to listen. People are not aware that their speaking can create problems instead of offering solutions. Yet they find it challenging to resist the urge to speak.

A person speaks excessively when they believe they have a lot of knowledge. This inclination is often driven by an ego-cantered urge to share their thoughts. A lack of curiosity is also a reason for speaking to fill conversational gaps. They neglect the importance of active listening. The feeling of insecurity is also another driving force behind excessive speaking. In this situation, an individual tries to get control and wants to address a threat through their spoken words. Those who are suffering from low self-control may feel it difficult to restrain themselves from speaking. They feel addicted to the compulsion to express their thoughts. The excessive speaking habit for instant gratification can create unhealthy communication. The habit of unnecessary speaking is nothing but an unnecessary overflow of words. If there is an absence of clarity and clear goals, there is a strong possibility of excessive speaking as a way to entertain oneself. There are so many people around you, they are only eager to speak and does not want to understand others' points of view. They only focus on responding, not on understanding. After doing that same thing frequently, they develop a habit of speaking too much.

Speaking can be a beneficial tool when you use it judiciously. When you don't have control over the urge to speak, you can face detrimental effects. This bad habit can be harmful in various ways. Excessive speaking diminishes your personal attraction. There will be no one who genuinely respects an excessively speaking person. Respect and trust may disappear when someone is a person of uncontrolled speaking. It raises doubts about their capabilities.

Excessive talking negatively impacts your learning capacity. The main reason is it diverts attention away from using all the senses effectively. The habit of speaking too much consumes both energy and willpower. It leaves you with low willpower and energy for productive work. Unconscious communication can make you more vulnerable because it provides others with information that can be used against you. If you hurt someone through your uncontrolled speech, it can fill you with guilt and shame. The habit of speaking excessively goes against social adaptation. It hinders the ability to connect meaningfully with others. If you are engaging in long and unnecessary conversations, it is nothing but wasting time. Now, it is time for some "Gray to Gold" ways to practice self-control while speaking.

Remember, there is no limit to knowledge and what you know is just a small part of it. Never think you know enough. Everyone has something specific to share. Always remember: Listening more is learning more, and learning more is earning more.

Only a good listener can be a good speaker. If you want to be a good speaker, first be a good listener.

Speak less to boost your self-esteem and willpower.

A good communicator always listens to understand, not just to respond.

A good communicator knows when to speak and when to listen, how to start and stop, what to say and what not to say.

You should be clear about your purpose for speaking. Without purpose, it's an unhealthy activity.

Whatever you want to say, say it clearly. Don't create confusion with too many words. Speak to the point.

Humour is the main ingredient of effective communication. It is more important than knowledge. Use humour to be liked by others.

Many human actions have unconscious origins. Speaking is also a part of unconscious behaviour. Speak with consciousness to avoid regretting what you say.

You must consider others before yourself. Speak about what suits the audience. You should share what is appreciated by others.

## Self-Affirmations

I am ................................. and I know that knowledge is limitless and what I know is just a fraction. I aspire to be a good speaker. I understand the importance of being a good listener. I choose to speak less because I know that it boosts my self-esteem and self-control. I am aware of when to speak and when to listen. I know how to start and stop. I am smart enough to know what to say and what not to say. I always express myself clearly. I acknowledge the importance of humour in effective communication. I use humour to connect with others. I speak with consciousness and avoid regrettable words.

*"To effectively communicate, we must realize that we are all different in the way we perceive the world and use this understanding as a guide to our communication with others."*
*- Tony Robbins*

# Impress Yourself

*"What you think of yourself is much more important than what others think of you."* - Seneca

Everyone tries to create a good status in society. A person with a good status always receives some extra advantages from society. It is a common desire to secure a good position among those around. There is nothing wrong with that because progress is an individual's birthright. Problems arise when a person chooses the wrong path. There are many ways that lead to destruction. Here in this chapter, we will discuss the way of "impressing others". An impression is an idea, a feeling, or an opinion that a person forms about self and somebody else. It is generally the process of image creation.

First of all, we will try to understand the psychology behind "impressing others". As social beings, humans want approval and acceptance from others. They want to impress others to gain recognition, validation, and a sense of importance within society. It is also a way for an individual to boost their self-esteem and secure their self-worth. When someone is admired or respected by others it provides them with a sense of confidence and validation. The desire to impress others can also originate from the need to influence or gain advantages in personal or professional life. When an individual feels insecure in society or within a particular group, they may try to impress others to compensate for their self-perceived weaknesses.

As we all know, excess of everything is bad. You will see many examples of people around you trying excessively to impress others. They are willing to do almost anything for that purpose. They showcase both tangible and intangible possessions. They always try to display physical assets like big houses, luxury cars, and more. They also try to encash their knowledge to grab someone's attention. Throughout this process of impressing others, they only get instant gratification. This instant gratification holds little significance in their life. At last, they feel, they have lost both physical and emotional resources in the way of impressing others.

A person who impatiently tries to impress others may lose themselves in this game. In the process, they lose connection with their true self. They could not explore their life in their desired way. Their confidence, willpower, self-esteem, self-love, and self-care may deteriorate with each action taken by them to impress others. That is why it becomes essential to recognize that you should not try to make everyone happy by suppressing your own life.

Impress yourself to impress others. If you do so, it will bring you good results. Instead of focusing on impressing others, you should work on impressing yourself. This is the way you can get the updated version of yourself. You should work on self-improvement. You can enhance your health and appearance. You can learn new skills. You should always follow your inner voice. You should always put effort into achieving your dreams and desires. This is the way you can explore your inner abilities. When you are only working to impress yourself, you can sustain your self-care and self-love. This act of self-impression will enhance your confidence, willpower, and self-esteem.

## Self-Affirmations

I am…………………………….. and I impress myself to bring out the best version of me. I don't focus on impressing others. I don't spend my energy and resources on impressing others. I always impress myself with self-care and self-love. I invest my efforts only in achieving my dreams and desires. I strongly believe that the way to impressing myself enhances my confidence, willpower, and self-esteem. I understand that impressing myself is the best way to impress others.

> *"To love oneself is the beginning of a lifelong romance."* - *Oscar Wilde*

# Safeguard secrets

*"Three may keep a secret if two of them are dead." - Benjamin Franklin*

*"A secret's worth depends on the people from whom it must be kept." - Carlos Ruiz Zafón*

In this complicated society of the present era, you need to create a special kind of protection, and that is keeping your secrets safe. The world is full of conflicts and hidden agendas. We are walking through unfamiliar territories of various predators. In this critical situation, rules are unclear, and ethics are often missing. There is a constant fight between those who could harm and those who could be harmed. One of the keys to surviving in the era of invisible enemies is having a shield of secrecy. This is a way to keep our vulnerabilities hidden. Here, speaking less is like you having a shield, and never revealing your secrets is the best protection you can have.

We are in the habit of sharing too much when we're so sad, happy or highly emotional. It can be risky. It is like a dangerous path because in that situation we reveal things that we should keep hidden. Social media platforms, and this online world made the circumstances more severe. On these internet platforms, sharing personal details can be even riskier. It becomes crucial to be smart enough about what we say or do in public and on the internet.

When we keep our plans or ideas to ourselves it helps us to stay strong and focused. Imagine, if you told everyone your plan to get what you want. Many might discourage you or even try to stop you. But if it's a secret until you achieve your goal, you have a better chance of success. Keeping secrets safe is also the foundation of having good and real friends. Not everyone needs to know everything about you. Some things are just for you, your close friends and family. You must have a special club where only a few people know each other.

Being secretive doesn't mean being alone or not trusting anyone. It's about being smart enough to choose when to share and when to keep things to yourself.

If you use it efficiently you are going to have an extra advantage that helps you to deal with various challenges of life. In this life, with lots of ups and downs, you must have a balance between sharing and keeping things to yourself. It is all about being wise, cautious, and aware of what you are doing. Enjoy this beautiful journey, but keep your secrets safe.

## Self-Affirmations

I am .................................... and I am mindful and conscious of my words and actions. My secrets are precious, and I value the strength that comes from keeping them safe. I choose to be silenced when needed. I understand that not every thought or secret deserves to be shared. My inner world is a sanctuary. I always avoid the temptation to share every detail on the public or digital platform. I know that not every battle needs to be fought in the open, some victories are quiet and personal. My secrets are like treasures and I ensure that they retain their value and significance. I carefully choose when and with whom to share the chapters of my life. I always appreciate the art of secrecy.

*"A secret's worth depends on the people from whom it must be kept." - Carlos Ruiz Zafón*

# Money Matters

*"The lack of money is the root of all evil." - Mark Twain*

Money is a vital part of our lives. It simplifies economic exchanges. It functions like blood in modern economies. It holds the power to make the world go around. While everyone uses money, only a few truly understand its nature and principles. Money has its value and acceptance; that is why it replaced the barter system. Unfortunately, many people consider money as evil. They associate it with crime and social issues. It's completely untrue and misguiding information. It is the unequal distribution of money and the ways people earn money that should be considered responsible. Money was and remains a useful tool for humanity. Without money, you cannot imagine the current economic development.

Money is like a friend as it helps us in different situations. It is important to understand how it works and the right way to treat it with respect. Money proves its friendship by being useful to us. That is why it is important to behave with money as we behave with a friend. To strengthen relationships with money, we can use it wisely and appreciate its support in our daily lives. Here I am mentioning some concepts related to money and suggesting some basic ways to make and manage friendship with money.

You must show gratitude for money as it greatly contributes to making your life easy. Expressing thanks to money forms a positive atmosphere that attracts more financial abundance. Gratitude for money is directly aligned with the principle of the 'law of attraction'. You must acknowledge and appreciate the role money plays in your daily life. You can create a welcoming atmosphere for its continued flow into your life.

Respecting money is a fundamental principle that enhances our financial understanding. Through this respect, you get to know about the real value of money. It is crucial to spend money wisely. One must reserve it for genuine needs rather than unmindful expenditures. Money, if treated with care and respect becomes a valuable asset that can create a more stable and happy life for you.

You can make money by using two methods: earning and saving. There is no other way to get money. Here, saving involves investment. Saved money is like earned money. We work to earn money, but that is not enough. We must know the art of saving it. You can accumulate money by stopping unnecessary expenses. You must save as much money as possible by being mindful of your spending habits and making thoughtful financial decisions.

You must prioritize your expenses. This practice ensures that your hard-earned money is used for the right reasons. Stick to the rule of priority in your life. You should make wise and meaningful use of your money.

Right conduct with money is the right investment of it. Making the right investments is the way through which money grows and generates more money.

You must also know the source of money. You should be aware of where your earnings come from. The source of money should be honest and legal. You must avoid choosing shortcuts or illegitimate ways to earn money.

Money should not be used to buy any form of addiction. It hurts money when we use it to buy unhealthy things. Addiction is one of the worst things you can spend your money on. Also, you should not give even a single penny to anyone for purchasing any type of addiction.

You must try to be self-dependent on money as soon as possible. When you use self-earned money, it gives you a sense of satisfaction and boosts your confidence. If you rely on others' money, it can make you feel low.

Just like any other form of education, financial education is also important in this time. You must consider reading financial education books. You can go for 'Rich Dad Poor Dad', 'Psychology of Money' and 'Think and Grow Rich,' and many others if you prefer.

You must build a strong belief that earning money doesn't necessarily require hard work; instead, it needs smart work. You should avoid working without using your wisdom. You can plan your work first to develop a strong and reliable system that will bring more money into your pocket.

You should not be a part of the crowd; instead, try to be unique and generate new ideas for your work. If you want to earn more money, you must start your venture instead of relying solely on a salary.

You should not show off that you have money. There is no need to build big houses and buy luxury cars. Don't create liabilities that drain your pocket and make you financially vulnerable. It is ok to have a house and car, but there is no need to spend excessively on them.

You must avoid the habit of 'land and spend money'. It can lead to big financial losses and deteriorated financial goodwill. Instead, create the habit of 'first earn, then save and then spend'. This approach will create a strong foundation for your financial stability through responsible money management.

When you step outside your house, you will encounter many people with greedy eyes on your pocket. Their aim is to transfer your money to their pockets through various techniques. You must be cautious and don't let them succeed in their bad intentions. If it is genuinely necessary, then only you should help otherwise there is no need to make a fool out of yourself. Protect your money from opportunists and manipulators.

Stay aware of advertisement industries. As I mentioned earlier, they are adept at manipulating your financial decisions.

Only purchase those items that you need genuinely in your life. There is no need to fall into the trap of unnecessary expenses.

In this era of uncertainty, where nothing is permanent and everything keeps changing, you should avoid financial vulnerability by developing multiple sources of income. Diversify your earning sources to ensure greater stability in unpredictable times.

In the 21st century, it is very important to acquire knowledge about the share market, mutual funds, stock exchange, and other financial instruments. You must understand these elements for financial literacy and the complex nature of modern finance.

You must avoid being overly money-centric. Money helps us deal with various situations and plays the role of a true friend in our lives. But always remember that excessive dependence on money can be unfavourable. When money occupies too much space in our lives, it can be detrimental to our overall social well-being. You should create a balance of money with other aspects of life.

Earning money is not a difficult task, but holding onto it can be challenging. Anyone can acquire money, but it takes wisdom to retain it. A foolish person always spends money on buying luxuries and instant pleasures. This way, he himself drains his account. Instead, a wise person invests money intelligently. This way, he generates more money and achieves financial independence.

Life is full of ups and downs. If you have your savings, it can provide you significant support in hard times. You must also have financial plans for every stage of your life. If you wisely manage your finances, it will ensure a more secure and stable future for you.

## Self-Affirmations

I am ………………………….. and I attract money into my life effortlessly. My financial success is a reflection of my positive attitude. I am in control of my finances. I make the right decisions that lead to prosperity. Money is a tool that allows me to live a happy and healthy life. I use it wisely for the benefit of myself and others. I am open to receiving wealth and I welcome opportunities for financial growth and success. I always treat money as my best friend.

> *"Too many people spend money they haven't earned, to buy things they don't want, to impress people they don't like."*
> *- Will Rogers*

# Path of Gratitude

*"Gratitude makes sense of our past, brings peace for today, and creates a vision for tomorrow." - Melody Beattie*

Gratitude is not just an act but a journey toward a more balanced and meaningful life. As we choose the way of gratitude, we open ourselves to the countless benefits and blessings. It transforms our lives and the lives of those around us. Gratitude is the most beautiful way of living life. Live a life where every moment is full of gratitude. We understand that we do all actions to achieve happiness. For all these actions, gratitude becomes the pathway that leads to happiness and joy. When we experience gratitude, we experience unending happiness which is already within us. The gratitude is so pure that its taste and essence cannot be described in words. A life full of gratitude resembles a garden full of beautiful flowers. Moments of intense gratitude are the most valuable moments of our lives.

When we get is what we desire, and express gratitude to the source, it creates an environment of peace and happiness. In our day-to-day lives, so many things and people assist or help us. There are countless blessings that come without any cost from the Mother Nature. When we face any challenging situations, the supernatural power shows us the way. Whatever possessions we have are not ours, they are given to us and we must express thanks and be grateful. Farmers grow crops to feed us, drivers transport our luggage and us, doctors take care of our health, and teachers inculcate true and useful knowledge. The Supreme Power has gifted us the most precious gift, life. It is a law of nature that gratitude brings more good things into our lives. It is our moral duty to develop the habit of saying thanks and showing gratitude. Communication full of gratitude gestures is always fruitful. God or the Supreme Power only wants gratitude from us and is ready to give anything to us if we express it. Gratitude protects us against all forms of negativity whether it is from negative people, experiences, emotions, feelings or circumstances.

Numerous studies have highlighted the psychological benefits of gratitude. Research shows that practicing gratitude can reduce stress, increase happiness, and improve overall mental and physical health. When we focus on what we are thankful for, we shift our attention from negative thoughts to positive ones. Studies have linked gratitude with better sleep, reduced illness, and improved health. In relationships, expressing gratitude can help us in creating strong connections both personally and professionally. Case studies reveal that gratitude often leads to healthy interactions and mutual respect.

Many times we get opportunities to show gratitude on various occasions and events. But the journey to maintaining gratefulness is not without obstacles. Difficult life circumstances and ingrained negative thinking patterns can negatively impact one's ability to feel grateful.

Saying "thanks" is not the only method of showing gratitude. Gratitude is a very broad concept and there are so many ways to express it. You can show gratitude by being kind to others, helping others, giving to others, showing respect to others, feeling love for others, maintaining a positive attitude toward others, and sharing good times with others. Gratitude has a deep and profound meaning. It feels like "life without gratitude is life without life". Gratitude is life within life, that keeps us humble and happy all times.

Each day we should start and end with gratitude. After waking up, we should express our gratitude and before going to sleep at night must repeat the same. We can remember those who made the day better for us. You can find real-life examples and stories around you, which illustrate how gratitude can transform lives. Always remember that Gratitude turns challenges into opportunities.

## Self-Affirmations

I am……………………………….. and I am grateful to God for giving me a wonderful life. I am also grateful to nature for providing everything that I need. The beauty of nature fills my soul with gratitude. I appreciate the unconditional love and support from my parents. I am thankful to my teachers who inspire and empower me. I feel thankful for the friends who bring joy, cooperation, and laughter into my life. I am thankful for my healthy body and brain that support me. I am grateful for the abundance of experiences and opportunities. I express gratitude for the financial prosperity. I acknowledge the correlated blessings of God, nature, family, teachers, friends, health, and wealth in my life.

*"Gratitude is the healthiest of all human emotions. The more you express gratitude for what you have, the more likely you will have even more to express gratitude for." - Zig Ziglar*

# Inhale and Exhale

*"When the breath is unsteady, all is unsteady; when the breath is still; all is still." - Hatha Yoga Pradipika*

In all living creatures the act of breathing is common. Breathing is an essential function that sustains life. Breathing involves the intake of oxygen, and with its help transforming food and water into energy that supplies power to all the functions of the body. Right breathing keeps us active, energetic, and healthy. Breathing is directly related to our consciousness, thinking, calmness, the ability to work physically and mentally, emotions, feelings and life on a large scale. To maintain these aspects of life in order, it becomes crucial to understand the art of breathing.

Breathing is a constant and unconscious activity. During moments of pain and anxiety, individuals may feel changes in their breathing patterns. In such circumstances, rapid, shallow breathing becomes common. Shallow breathing involves the chest instead of the stomach. Shallow breathing creates an irregular heart rate, high blood pressure, muscular tension, and the release of stress hormones. Shallow breathing is directly correlated with stress, anxiety, and depression. These signals sent by shallow breathing create an emergency-like situation for the body and brain and that trigger unnecessary and chaotic defence mechanisms of the brain and body.

Mastering the art of breathing is not a hard task; instead, it is a skill that can be easily acquired. A person who, by practicing conscious breathing reduces the breaths to five times or less per minute is now the master of this art. Anyone can gain control over this profound art by using a very simple trick. Divide the breath into four parts: inhaling, holding, exhaling, and holding again. Each part should last for four seconds. It's important to initiate the breath from the stomach, not from the chest. Also, breathe in and out through the nose, not through the mouth. The beauty of learning the art of conscious breathing lies in its flexibility. You can practice it anywhere and at any time.

Taking this practice to a deeper level involves associating positive and negative things with inhalation and exhalation. You can feel abundance, love, peace, and happiness coming with inhaling, and during exhaling, you can feel the release of fear, sadness, anxiety, anger, and suffering. In my point of view, this is one of the best manifestation techniques.

The practice of slow and deep breathing finds its roots in ancient Indian and Buddhist traditions. It is trusted by saints and monks for the mental, physical, emotional and spiritual well-being. Physical instructors and yoga teachers use these techniques to empower the strength and stamina of their followers significantly. Controlled, deep, and slow breathing techniques have the potential to optimize brain and body functions. It promotes health, happiness, and overall well-being of a person who knows the importance of this art and follows it.

## Self-Affirmations:

I am ………………………………….and I firmly believe in the power of slow and deep breathing. I am a master of this wonderful art. I breathe fewer than five times per minute. I always sense the origin of breath in my stomach. I inhale and exhale through my nose. With each inhale, I welcome positivity, and with each exhale, I release negativity. I strongly believe that I am a conscious breather.

*"Inhale the future, exhale the past." - Unknown*

# Books Worth Reading

*"Books are a uniquely portable magic." - Stephen King*

The interest in reading books is crucial in this era of uncertainty. Books are among the most powerful tools to face the uncertainty of the 21st century. Books are the reservoirs of knowledge and experiences. Books offer you guidance for learning new skills. You can learn both personal and professional skills by reading books. Books provide a well-trusted, systematic approach to understanding the various aspects of life. Reading more and more books allows you to gain applicable insights into your life.

Books are the main source of your self-reflection. Books offer practical advice and equip you with powerful skills to face challenges effectively. You can ensure your personal growth by learning and applying the principles from various books.

Knowledge inherited from books builds your self-esteem and creates a healthy environment for your overall well-being. You get practical, applicable, and fruitful strategies for personal development from reading books. There are only books that provide you with true wisdom. You can get well-researched and scientific advice from books. Books help you learn more with less energy and resources. Books play the role of guides. Books are one of the best tools to enhance your potential and capabilities. You can create good habits to deal with various aspects of life successfully with the help of books.

Here, I am suggesting you some "Gray to Gold" books. You can start your journey of self-discovery and growth with this collection of books. You can explore the power of consciousness and gratitude to unlock your overall well-being. These books will help you in the creation of good habits. These books will offer you a diverse range of insights. Here I am suggesting this collection of ten books. I strongly believe that you will get practical insights for facing the complex nature of life in this era. Each book will prove to be a valuable companion on your journey of self-improvement. I also believe that these books will offer you wisdom to empower your actions and reactions in dealing with the challenges of the 21st century.

## The Secret

This is a book written by Rhonda Byrne that explores the concept of the law of attraction. It was published in 2006. The book explains the law of attraction. It suggests that positive thinking can attract positive outcomes into your life. The writer explains the idea that thoughts are like magnets for circumstances. The book also shares insights from various philosophers, thinkers, and successful individuals to clarify the law of attraction. It also explains the power of gratitude and its role in your life. You must read, reread, and keep reading this book throughout your life. "The Greatest Secret" by the same writer is the second half of this book. You must also read this book to understand the role of consciousness, mind, resentment, and acceptance.

## The Peaceful Warrior

This book is written by Dan Millman. It's a spiritual novel that is a mixture of fiction with autobiographical elements. It was published in 1980. The book follows the journey of the writer himself as a college gymnast. The writer randomly meets a mysterious gas station attendant named Socrates. Socrates has a series of conversations with him full of teachings. Socrates teaches life lessons and philosophy to Dan millman. He guides him on a path of self-discovery and personal transformation. By reading this book, you will learn about the importance of living in the present moment. It is a complete saga of three books by Dan Millman that covers the full story. The journey of Socrates is my favourite.

## How to Win Friends and Influence People

This book is written by Dale Carnegie and is my all-time favourite. It provides valuable insights into effective communication and relationship building. By reading this book, you will understand the importance of communication in your life. You will get to know about various things about human behaviour. You will learn through this book the best communication skills. After reading this book, you will be a master in communication and relationship building. The book is full of wonderful concepts that can empower you to have positive, strong, and respectful conversations.

## Sapiens: A Brief History of Humankind

This book is written by Yuval Noah Harari. It provides a holistic approach to understanding the history of Homo sapiens from the emergence of our species to the present day. The writer explores key milestones in human development. These milestones are the Cognitive Revolution, Agricultural Revolution, and the formation of empires. By reading this book, you will understand how cultural, social, and technological changes have shaped human societies. By reading this book, you can understand history and the impact of individual and collective human actions on the world.

## Deep Work

This book was authored by Cal Newport and published in 2016. This book is about the concept of deep work. Deep work is defined as the ability to concentrate on tasks without distraction. The writer highlights the difference between deep work and shallow work. There is a scarcity of deep work in today's distracted world. The book suggests deep work for higher productivity with better quality work. In this book, he highlights how the ability to engage in deep work is crucial for professional success in this era.

## The Power of Habit

This book is authored by Charles Duhigg and published in 2012. It explains habits and neuroscience of habit formation. It explains how habits become ingrained in our brains and shape our behaviour on a subconscious level. The insights of this book also cover business and organizational habits. Overall, by reading this book, we understand the importance of habits. It is valuable for readers who are seeking personal and professional growth.

## Lifespan: Why We Age – and Why We Don't Have To

This book is authored by Dr. David Sinclair and was published in 2019. It explores the science of ageing. The writer discusses the molecular and cellular factors that cause ageing. The book suggests that dietary changes, physical workouts and other good habits can positively impact cellular health. This book explains not only the current scientific progress but also looks toward future advancements. There could be a possible revolution in our ability to slow down or reverse the ageing process.

## Rich Dad Poor Dad

This book is authored by Robert T. Kiyosaki and was published in 1997. It offers valuable insights into financial literacy. It explains fundamental concepts such as assets versus liabilities. It shows the importance of acquiring income-generating assets. The book explains how to build wealth through investments. It finds the traditional education system incompetent in financial literacy. The author supports an entrepreneurial mindset. He encourages readers to take calculated risks. It is a bestseller and inspires many to achieve financial independence.

## Zen: The Art of Simple Living

This book is authored by Shunmyo Masuno, a Japanese Zen Buddhist priest. He guides readers toward a simple and satisfied life. The book includes principles of minimalism and simplicity. The book is full of wonderful and practical advice rooted in Zen philosophy. The ultimate goal of this book is to inspire you to mindful daily rituals. It also helps you in establishing a deeper connection with the present.

## The 5 AM Club

This book was written by Robin Sharma and published in 2018. The author explores the transformative power of the habit of waking up early. The book explains the positive impact of adopting the 5 AM Club principles on personal development. After reading the book, you will understand that waking up early is a catalyst for your increased productivity and overall well-being. There are many practical insights intermingled in the story that can create positive changes in your life.

## Self-Affirmations

I am……………………………….and I embrace the habit of reading books. I recognize books as a powerful tool for self-discovery and self-empowerment. Every book I read is a step forward toward an updated version of myself. I strengthen my perspectives and deepen my understanding of all aspects of life by reading books. Reading books is my conscious choice to invest in my personal growth. It leads me toward a life of peace and happiness. I believe that reading books is an act of self-care.

*"I cannot live without books." - Thomas Jefferson*

# Movies Worth Watching

*"Movies touch our hearts, awaken our vision, and change the way we see things. They take us to other places; they open doors and minds." - Martin Scorsese*

I think we all enjoy watching movies. Whether more or less, everyone is interested in them. It's not just entertainment, but we also learn a lot through movies without even realizing it. When we feel negative and exhausted, we watch movies to become positive and to recharge. Watching good movies relaxes the brain and body and provide a useful escape from reality. It allows us to explore different societies, diverse cultures, geographical landmarks, and history. We feel emotions and understand human behaviour. Good movies can serve as a source of real motivation. Good movies are full of inspiration, innovation, creativity, and healthy conversations. Watching movies can increase the brain's activity by enhancing visual and auditory processing skills. Cinematography is a powerful medium for storytelling. Movies are the best medium for conveying complex ideas, thoughts, narratives, feelings, and emotions. It also helps bringing people together by creating common feelings.

Here, I suggest a list of ten movies or documentaries which cover various aspects of life. I hope that this list will offer you both entertainment and opportunities. I believe you will learn new insights and understand the pluralistic nature of the world.

## The Secret: Dare to Dream

This is a 2020 romantic drama film directed by Andy Tennant. It is based on the self -help book "The Secret" by Rhonda Byrne. The film aims to convey inspirational and spiritual messages. It signifies the power of thoughts in shaping one's life. It explores the potential for positive change in the face of adversity through shifting thoughts. This movie clarifies the concept of the law of attraction. This movie displays the role of gratitude and positive thinking in our lives.

## The Peaceful Warrior

This is a 2006 film directed by Victor Salva. This movie is based on the novel "Way of the Peaceful Warrior" by Dan Millman. The movie combines insights with spirituality. It stars Scott Mechlowicz as Dan Millman and Nick Nolte as his spiritual guide, Socrates. The film explores the concept of pursuit of excellence and happiness, the importance of living in the present moment, and the power of awareness and consciousness. If you want to watch something useful for your personal growth, "Peaceful Warrior" might be the best choice.

## Pursuit of Happiness

This film was directed by Gabriele Muccino. It's based on the true story of Chris Gardner, a struggling salesman. While raising his young son, he was suffering from homelessness. This inspirational movie highlights strong willpower, determination, and the pursuit of dreams against all odds. It can inspire you for your personal growth. It emphasizes the importance of perseverance, determination, optimistic thinking, and the belief that work done in the right way can lead to success.

## 3 Idiots

This is a popular Indian film directed by Rajkumar Hirani. It revolves around three friends at an engineering college. The movie explores concept of pursuing one's passion, questioning social expectations, and the importance of holistic education. It will encourage you to think about prioritizing personal happiness and self-discovery over social expectations.

## The Matrix

This is a science fiction film released in 1999 and directed by the Wachowskis. It explores the concept of a simulated reality controlled by machines and humans are unaware of their true existence. The protagonist discovers the truth and joins a group of rebels fighting against the machines. This movie offers several thought-provoking questions and lessons. This movie discusses issues and concepts like reality perception, freedom from machines, the power of technology, self-consciousness, and philosophical concepts such as existentialism.

## The Boy Who Harnessed the Wind

This film was released in 2019, directed by and starring Chiwetel Ejiofor. The movie is based on the true story of William Kamkwamba, a young Malawian boy. During a severe famine in his village, he built a wind turbine and brought electricity to his community. The film portrays William's determination to overcome challenges and pursue education against all odds. It highlights the power of real education in transforming lives. It is among the best examples where one person's resourcefulness can make a significant impact on a community facing adversity.

## The Martian

This is a science fiction film released in 2015 and directed by Ridley Scott. It is based on the novel of the same name by Andy Weir. The film stars Matt Damon as Mark Watney, an astronaut. He is isolated on Mars after his crew assumes he is dead during a severe dust storm. The movie revolves around Watney's struggle for survival on Mars. He uses his scientific knowledge, willpower, and resourcefulness to overcome challenges and find a way to communicate with Earth. "The Martian" provides viewers with insights into the power of humour to overcome obstacles.

## Trapped

This movie was released in 2016 and directed by Vikramaditya Motwane. Rajkummar Rao in the lead role gets trapped in his apartment in a high-rise building in Mumbai. The story unfolds as he struggles to survive without water, food and electricity. The film is known for depicting the psychological and physical challenges faced by the protagonist. It shares psychological impact of isolation, resourcefulness, the value of basic things, and the human instinct to survive under odd circumstances.

## The Social Dilemma

This is a documentary that explores the impact of social media on society. It discusses issues like addiction, misinformation, and privacy concerns inherited in social media. It spreads awareness about the consequences of social media platforms. The documentary includes interviews with former employees of big tech giants. It also highlights the efforts to increase user engagement and the manipulation of online behaviour. This documentary raises a voice for the need for ethical considerations in the development of social media platforms.

## Hitler: A Career

This documentary was released in 1977. It is about the rise and fall of Adolf Hitler. It was directed by Christian Herrendoerfer and Joachim Fest. It was written by Fest, a German historian. It provides insights into history and shows how an ordinary person becomes a dictator who is responsible for the death of 6 million Jews and millions others worldwide. The documentary depicts Hitler's real role in World War II and the atrocities committed during the Holocaust. It also provides insights into political climate and the impact of political propaganda on the world. If you have access to the documentary, go and watch it. It can offer you a comprehensive understanding of this dark period in history and insightful learnings from it.

## Self-Affirmations

I am……………………………………and I believe in the idea that watching good movies is a powerful tool for learning and self-empowerment. I have the ability to learn valuable insights and lessons from well-crafted films. I release any guilt in enjoying movies. I recognize the real positive force of insightful movies. Movies makes me aware of diverse cultures, crucial lessons from history, various experiences, human nature, and all the good and bad possibilities of the world. Watching good movies empowers me to deal with various aspects of my life.

*"The cinema is not an art which films life: the cinema is something between art and life. Unlike painting and literature, the cinema both gives to life and takes from it." - Jean-Luc Godard*

www.ingramcontent.com/pod-product-compliance
Lightning Source LLC
LaVergne TN
LVHW041938070526
838199LV00051BA/2835